פרקי אבות וברכת המזון

pirkei avos
and
Bircas
hamazon

ETHICS OF THE FATHERS
AND GRACE AFTER MEALS/

A NEW TRANSLATION WITH A CONCISE
COMMENTARY ANTHOLOGIZED FROM
THE CLASSICAL RABBINIC SOURCES.

Commentary by
Rabbi Meir Zlotowitz

Overview by
Rabbi Nosson Schermam

Published by
Mesorah Publications, ltd

FESTIVAL

PIRKEI AVOS AND BIRCAS HAMAZON
FIRST EDITION
Seven Impressions ... June 1999 — April 2008
SECOND EDITION
Six Impressions ... April 2010 — February 2021

Published and Distributed by
MESORAH PUBLICATIONS, LTD.
313 Regina Avenue / Rahway, N.J 07065

Distributed in Europe by
LEHMANNS
Unit E, Viking Business Park
Rolling Mill Road
Jarow, Tyne & Wear, NE32 3DP
England

Distributed in Australia and New Zealand by
GOLDS WORLDS OF JUDAICA
3-13 William Street
Balaclava, Melbourne 3183
Victoria, Australia

Distributed in Israel by
SIFRIATI / A. GITLER — BOOKS
POB 2351
Bnei Brak 51122

Distributed in South Africa by
KOLLEL BOOKSHOP
Northfield Centre, 17 Northfield Avenue
Glenhazel 2192, Johannesburg, South Africa

ARTSCROLL® MESORAH SERIES
PIRKEI AVOS AND BIRCAS HAMAZON /
ETHICS OF THE FATHERS AND GRACE AFTER MEALS

© Copyright 1984, 1999, by MESORAH PUBLICATIONS, Ltd.
313 Regina Avenue / Rahway, N.J. 07065 / (718) 921-9000 / www.artscroll.com

---

ALL RIGHTS RESERVED

*The text, prefatory and associated textual contents and introductions
— including the typographic layout, cover artwork and ornamental graphics —
have been designed, edited and revised as to content, form and style.*

**No part of this book may be reproduced
IN ANY FORM, PHOTOCOPING, OR COMPUTER RETRIEVAL SYSTEMS
— even for personal use without written permission from
the copyright holder, Mesorah Publications Ltd.**
*except by a reviewer who wishes to quote brief passages
in connection with a review written for inclusion in magazines or newspapers.*

THE RIGHTS OF THE COPYRIGHT HOLDER WILL BE STRICTLY ENFORCED.

ISBN 10: 1-57819-266-8 / 978-1-57819-266-3 (color cover)
ISBN 10: 1-57819-267-6 / 978-1-57819-267-0 (pearl white cover)

Typography by CompuScribe at ArtScroll Studios, Ltd.
Printed in the United States of America by Noble Book Press

An Overview /
Avos — the Doorway to Torah and Life

The cloak of wintry darkness is lifting and the late setting sun beckons man to enjoy the unfolding glories of nature. Passover is gone and Shavuos — the festival of revelation, the festival that gives meaning to the freedom of the Exodus — is on its way. In their homes, synagogues, and study halls, Jews open their hearts to *Pirkei Avos / Ethics of the Fathers*, the only tractate of the Mishnah that is not halachic in nature.

Not in *Avos* are the laws of Sabbath labor or the Temple Service, the exacting logic of civil or marriage law, or the intricate *halachos* of agriculture or ritual purity. *Avos* is filled with rules of moral conduct, maxims of ethical behavior, pithy formulations of wise guidance in everyday life. Yet in the truest sense, this non-halachic book is the prerequisite to the Halachah itself.

In the truest sense, this non-halachic book is the prerequisite to the Halachah itself.

How is *Avos* unique? Why was it chosen for recitation during the long summer afternoons? How is it different from and preferable to other collections of sayings by wise and pious leaders? Why is it called *Avos*, Fathers?

People, Not Animals

Someone once asked Rabbi Yitzchok Ze'ev Soleveitchick, the last rabbi of pre-Holocaust Brisk, Lithuania: "The Talmud and Rabbinic literature lay great stress on character and ethics. We are told that an uncontrolled temper is like idolatry; shaming a fellow human being is akin to bloodshed; God so abhors an arrogant person that He cannot abide in the same universe with the haughty. The list of such teachings is endless — but if they are truly so important, why are the requirements of good character and ethics not listed among the 613 commandments of the Torah?"

In the concise and incisive manner for which he was famous, the Brisker Rav replied, "The Torah was given to people, not animals. Only by controlling and conquering the animal within oneself can a person become worthy of the wisdom and requirements of the Torah."

This idea is as old as the Torah itself. True service of God and obedience to the teaching of the Torah demand that a person rid himself of the selfishness that filters duty, people, and morality through the prism of self-interest. Let us imagine the reactions of two different people — one coarse, the other refined — to the Talmudic passage:

> R' Yehudah said: One who wishes to be devout, let him fulfill his teaching of Nezikin [the section of the Talmud that deals with torts and civil law] (Bava Kamma 30a).

A base person would study these laws very carefully so that he will know how to protect his own interest and how to evade responsibility for his actions. He will learn how to plead and argue, how to use contractual language that will give him maximum protection at the expense of his fellows. On the other hand, a person who has taken on the hard task of improving himself will study *Nezikin* for the very opposite reason. He will exert himself to be sure that he causes no injury to the property or interest of others, that he retains not a penny to which another human being has a just claim. Obviously, when the Talmud hinges devotion and piety on the study of these laws, it presupposes that it is indeed speaking to "people, not animals," that the person opening the intricate legal tomes of *Nezikin* is doing so to discover God's rules of fair dealing and property rights, not to find ways to twist the letter of the law into a web that ensnares innocent victims.

A person who has taken on the hard task of improving himself will study Nezikin to be sure that he causes no injury to others.

Devotion Through Law

No doubt this is why the same Talmudic passage goes on to quote Rava who declares that one who wished to be devout should study *Avos*, the small tractate that is filled with the ethical and moral exhortations of the Sages. By building his character on the teachings of *Avos*, one lifts himself out of the jungle where personal survival and success are the paramount, perhaps the only, values. Such a person sees *Nezikin* from a truly humane and devout perspective.

Such a person sees Nezikin from a truly humane and devout perspective.

He sees the world from the viewpoint of the Chofetz Chaim. Once the saint and sage was a passenger in a horse-drawn cart when the driver, with larceny in his heart, was irresistibly drawn to some unguarded bales of hay on a roadside farm. Reining in his horses, the driver peered carefully in all directions to see if anyone was watching and then, seeing that he was unobserved, ran to load a few bales onto his wagon.

The Chofetz Chaim shouted to him, "Reb Yid, they are watching, they are watching!"

The Doorway to Torah and Life **[4]**

Without hesitation the driver dropped his quarry and leaped onto the wagon for a quick getaway. As his horses galloped away to safety, the driver looked over his shoulder and was surprised to see that no one was pursuing him! Angrily, he demanded that the Chofetz Chaim tell him who was watching. Serenely, the Chofetz Chaim pointed to the sky and said, "*They* are watching!"

> To the "wagon drivers" of the world, property rights are determined by watchmen and witnesses.

To the "wagon drivers" of the world, property rights are determined by watchmen and witnesses. To the Chofetz Chaims of the world, the admonition of *Avos* is sufficient: Consider three things and you will not come into the grip of sin: know what is above you — a watchful eye ... (2:1).

A person imbued with the lessons of *Avos* will have different goals than one conditioned by the grasping, bottom-line, me-first mentality that colors society's most popular road maps to success. Clearly, there is a spiritual nobility in people who live according to such lessons of *Avos* as Hillel's: "Do not judge your fellow until your have reached his place" (2:5); or Rabban Yochanan ben Zakkai's: "If you have studied much Torah, do not take credit for yourself, because that is what you were created to do" (2:9).

Angels Among Men

Let no one think, however, that the lessons of *Avos* are merely the moral preachings of noble but mortal men. If it were nothing more than that, *Avos* would be comparable to many other books of maxims and manuals of self-improvement. Wise people in all the world's cultures have charted paths to perfection that crisscross wildly in different and often conflicting directions. True, intelligence is the indispensable tool to perfection, but unless it has a guiding philosophy it is like a powerful motor without a steering mechanism. Every field of endeavor has been filled with good and bright people who were dismal failures or grotesque successes because they lacked moral rudders to direct their considerable talents.

> The teachings of *Avos* are the accumulated wisdom of people who dedicated their lives to the service of God and the study of His Torah.

The teachings of *Avos* are the accumulated wisdom of people who dedicated their lives to the service of God and the study of His Torah. Such people embodied in intellect and deed what God had in mind when He said, "Let us make man in Our image after Our likeness." In the perceptive, poetic words of Rabbi Avrohom Yeshaya Karelitz:

> *The human being who is privileged to know the Torah — meaning that the intellect placed in his soul, like a seed in the furrow of a field, unites with*

> *his knowledge and they become a single entity — walks among people and seems to any superficial observer like an ordinary person. But! — in truth he is an angel dwelling among mortal men, and he lives a life of spiritual ecstasy that is exalted above all blessing and praise (Kovetz Iggaros, Chazon Ish 1:13).*

One does not ask accountants to train artists, or vice versa. So, too, only the great Torah figures could draw the moral road map.

Only the accomplished practitioners of any craft can set forth the rules for successful pursuit of their calling; one does not ask accountants to train artists, or vice versa. So, too, only the great Torah figures could draw the moral road map for the quest after human perfection as God defines it in the Torah. This is why *Avos* is not only authoritative, but unique. Only here do "angels dwelling among mortal men" congregate to teach other mortal men to become angels. The Vilna Gaon shows how every teaching in this little tractate is based on Scripture and its Talmudic interpretation. Others may not go so far, but all commentators agree without exception that the teachings of *Avos* are powerfully rooted in the Torah itself. In Jewish tradition, one achieves acceptance as a great teacher by combining high degrees of Torah knowledge, piety, devotion to fellow men — all the qualities demanded of the *total* Jewish personality. The outlook of such people has a particular validity even when they offer no proof for their views, because inevitably their attitudes and thoughts are expressions of the study, goals, and values that molded them. Thus, for the nation of Torah, the aphorisms of a Hillel, a Rabban Yochanan ben Zakkai, and the other sages in *Avos* have the validity of God's Own word.

In Jewish tradition, one achieves acceptance as a great teacher by combining all the qualities demanded of the total Jewish personality.

Fathers and Principles

The tractate is called *Avos*, Fathers, a word that has two connotations. The obvious one is that a father is one who begets others, biologically or spiritually. The other is in the sense of first principle or primary rule, as we find in the Talmud, that the primary forms of forbidden Sabbath labor are called אֲבוֹת מְלָאכָה, literally "*fathers of labor.*" The name *Avos* in the case of our tractate has both connotations. It comprises the collective wisdom of the intellectual and spiritual fathers of our people. And their teachings constitute the primary principles of human behavior, as expected of the nation of the Torah.

It is quite understandable, therefore, that Jewish communities made the recitation and study of *Avos* a regular part of their lives beginning at least twelve centuries ago. In many communities, it was recited only during the Sabbaths from Pesach to Shavuos, as a fitting preparation for the festival of the Revelation at Sinai. For that reason, too, the sixth chapter, which deals with Torah study, was appended to the five chapters of *Avos* as a particularly appropriate recitation for the Sabbath before Shavuos. Another reason for beginning the recitation of *Avos* at that time of the year is that the period between Pesach and Shavuos saw the death of more than 20,000 of R' Akiva's students, the backbone of Judaism's scholarly community. The reason for this nearly mortal blow to our spiritual wellbeing was that they failed to honor one another properly, the sort of shortcoming that the lessons of *Avos* can counteract. Today's prevalent custom is to continue the weekly recitation until Rosh Hashanah, so that the long summertime Sabbath afternoons can be filled with shared Torah study.

There is yet another reason that the genius of the Jewish soul adopted the study of *Avos* for the full spring and summer season, a reason that is always pertinent. As the shroud of winter lifts and nature luxuriates in a new blossoming, it is all too natural for people to turn their minds to relaxation and pleasure. The elements beckon, why should we not enjoy them? When people relax their self-discipline, duty and morality are often early casualties. "Open the pages of *Avos*," our wise men counseled. "You need it all year, but never more than now."

This translation with commentary is taken from the full Weekday-Sabbath-Festival ArtScroll *Siddur*. It enables the reader to achieve a relatively quick grasp of the fundamentals of the tractate, and we present it in the hope that it will stimulate the reader to dig deeply in the rich lode of wisdom it represents.

> *As Ben Bag Bag said of the Torah to which Avos opens the door:*
> *Delve in the Torah and continue to delve in the Torah, for everything is in it; look deeply into it; grow old and gray over it, and do not stir from it, for you can have no better portion than it (5:26).*
>
> — Rabbi Nosson Scherman

פרק ראשון

א

כָּל יִשְׂרָאֵל יֵשׁ לָהֶם חֵלֶק לָעוֹלָם הַבָּא, שֶׁנֶּאֱמַר: "וְעַמֵּךְ כֻּלָּם צַדִּיקִים, לְעוֹלָם יִירְשׁוּ אָרֶץ, נֵצֶר מַטָּעַי, מַעֲשֵׂה יָדַי לְהִתְפָּאֵר."

❈ ❈ ❈

[א] מֹשֶׁה קִבֵּל תּוֹרָה מִסִּינַי, וּמְסָרָהּ לִיהוֹשֻׁעַ, וִיהוֹשֻׁעַ לִזְקֵנִים, וּזְקֵנִים לִנְבִיאִים, וּנְבִיאִים מְסָרוּהָ לְאַנְשֵׁי כְנֶסֶת הַגְּדוֹלָה. הֵם אָמְרוּ שְׁלֹשָׁה דְבָרִים: הֱווּ מְתוּנִים בַּדִּין, וְהַעֲמִידוּ תַלְמִידִים הַרְבֵּה, וַעֲשׂוּ סְיָג לַתּוֹרָה.

[ב] שִׁמְעוֹן הַצַּדִּיק הָיָה מִשְּׁיָרֵי כְנֶסֶת הַגְּדוֹלָה. הוּא הָיָה אוֹמֵר: עַל שְׁלֹשָׁה דְבָרִים הָעוֹלָם עוֹמֵד: עַל הַתּוֹרָה, וְעַל הָעֲבוֹדָה, וְעַל גְּמִילוּת חֲסָדִים.

[ג] אַנְטִיגְנוֹס אִישׁ סוֹכוֹ קִבֵּל מִשִּׁמְעוֹן הַצַּדִּיק. הוּא הָיָה אוֹמֵר: אַל תִּהְיוּ כַּעֲבָדִים הַמְשַׁמְּשִׁין אֶת הָרַב עַל מְנָת לְקַבֵּל פְּרָס; אֶלָּא הֱווּ כַּעֲבָדִים הַמְשַׁמְּשִׁין אֶת הָרַב שֶׁלֹּא עַל מְנָת לְקַבֵּל פְּרָס; וִיהִי מוֹרָא שָׁמַיִם עֲלֵיכֶם.

[ד] יוֹסֵי בֶן יוֹעֶזֶר אִישׁ צְרֵדָה וְיוֹסֵי בֶן יוֹחָנָן אִישׁ יְרוּשָׁלַיִם קִבְּלוּ מֵהֶם. יוֹסֵי בֶן יוֹעֶזֶר אִישׁ צְרֵדָה אוֹמֵר: יְהִי בֵיתְךָ בֵית וַעַד לַחֲכָמִים, וֶהֱוֵי מִתְאַבֵּק בַּעֲפַר רַגְלֵיהֶם, וֶהֱוֵי שׁוֹתֶה בַצָּמָא אֶת דִּבְרֵיהֶם.

CHAPTER ONE

◆§ Prologue

כָּל יִשְׂרָאֵל — *All Israel.* This maxim is taken from the Mishnah, *Sanhedrin* 90a. It is read as an introduction to each chapter of *Avos* because it increases our incentive to apply ourselves to the teachings of this tractate. Since our ultimate reward in the World to Come is within reach, why should we not pursue the ways to attain it?

The term *Israel* refers to any individual who has not utterly divorced himself from Israel's lofty spiritual and ethical destiny. His portion in the World to Come will vary according to his merit, but as long as he remains part of "Israel," he will never lose it entirely (R' Hirsch).

1. תּוֹרָה — *Torah.* The term Torah includes the Written Law (תּוֹרָה שֶׁבִּכְתָב), i.e., the Five Books of Moses), and the accompanying Oral Law (תּוֹרָה שֶׁבְּעַל פֶּה) — the interpretation of the Text as Divinely handed down to Moses in its entirety and expounded by successive generations of Sages. Moses received the Torah from God at Sinai in full view of all the people. The term מִסִּינַי, *from Sinai,* means from God Who appeared at Sinai. Moses expounded the Torah to them during the forty years of their wanderings through the desert, and before he died he "transferred" the tradition to Joshua to ensure its perpetuation.

אַנְשֵׁי כְנֶסֶת הַגְּדוֹלָה — *The Men of the Great Assembly.* This group of 120 Sages led

CHAPTER ONE

All Israel has a share in the World to Come, as it is said: "And your people are all righteous; they shall inherit the land forever; they are the branch of My planting, My handiwork, in which to take pride" (Isaiah 60:21).

❃ ❃ ❃

[1] **מֹשֶׁה** *Moses received the Torah from Sinai and transmitted it to Joshua; Joshua to the Elders; the Elders to the Prophets; and the Prophets transmitted it to the Men of the Great Assembly. They [the Men of the Great Assembly] said three things: Be deliberate in judgment; develop many disciples; and make a fence for the Torah.*

[2] *Shimon the Righteous was among the survivors of the Great Assembly. He used to say: The world depends on three things — on Torah study, on the service [of God], and on kind deeds.*

[3] *Antigonus, leader of Socho, received the tradition from Shimon the Righteous. He used to say: Be not like servants who serve their master for the sake of receiving a reward; instead be like servants who serve their master not for the sake of receiving a reward. And let the awe of Heaven be upon you.*

[4] *Yose ben Yoezer, leader of Tz'redah, and Yose ben Yochanan, leader of Jerusalem, received the tradition from them. Yose ben Yoezer, leader of Tz'redah, says: Let your house be a meeting place for sages; sit in the dust of their feet; and drink in their words thirstily.*

the Jewish people at the beginning of the Second Temple era. It included the last prophets, among them Ezra, Mordechai, Haggai, Zechariah, and Malachi. As the Sages put it, the Assembly "restored the crown of the Torah to its pristine splendor." They laid the foundation of the liturgy, edited several of the Scriptural Books, provided for the intensified study of the Oral Law, and enacted many ordinances designed to prevent laxity in observance of the commandments.

סְיָג לַתּוֹרָה — *A fence* [protective bounds] *for the Torah.* Enact provisions and cautionary rules to safeguard against transgression of the laws of the Torah itself. For example, the Rabbis forbade even the handling of certain utensils on the Sabbath (מוּקְצֶה), lest one use them to perform a labor forbidden by the Torah.

2. הָעֲבוֹדָה — *The service [of God],* i.e., the sacrificial service in the Temple and, in the absence of the Temple, study of the laws regarding the service. In its broader sense, *service* refers to prayer and the performance of the commandments.

גְּמִילוּת חֲסָדִים — *Kind deeds,* i.e., the performance of benevolent acts between man and his fellow.

3. אַל תִּהְיוּ כַּעֲבָדִים — *Be not like servants,* i.e., serve God out of love for Him, not merely because your good deeds will be rewarded.

מוֹרָא שָׁמַיִם — *Awe of Heaven.* This reverence must be maintained even though one have great love for God, for awe will inhibit one from transgressing His laws, while love not complemented by fear can sometimes lead one to take excessive liberties.

4. וֶהֱוֵי מִתְאַבֵּק בַּעֲפַר רַגְלֵיהֶם — *Sit in the dust of their feet.* Attend to their needs (*Rav*). In Mishnaic times, the teacher

[9] **PIRKEI AVOS** / CHAPTER 1

א [ה] יוֹסֵי בֶּן יוֹחָנָן אִישׁ יְרוּשָׁלַיִם אוֹמֵר: יְהִי בֵיתְךָ פָתוּחַ לִרְוָחָה, וְיִהְיוּ עֲנִיִּים בְּנֵי בֵיתֶךָ, וְאַל תַּרְבֶּה שִׂיחָה עִם הָאִשָּׁה. בְּאִשְׁתּוֹ אָמְרוּ, קַל וָחֹמֶר בְּאֵשֶׁת חֲבֵרוֹ. מִכַּאן אָמְרוּ חֲכָמִים: כָּל הַמַּרְבֶּה שִׂיחָה עִם הָאִשָּׁה — גּוֹרֵם רָעָה לְעַצְמוֹ, וּבוֹטֵל מִדִּבְרֵי תוֹרָה, וְסוֹפוֹ יוֹרֵשׁ גֵּיהִנֹּם.

[ו] יְהוֹשֻׁעַ בֶּן פְּרַחְיָה וְנִתַּאי הָאַרְבֵּלִי קִבְּלוּ מֵהֶם. יְהוֹשֻׁעַ בֶּן פְּרַחְיָה אוֹמֵר: עֲשֵׂה לְךָ רַב, וּקְנֵה לְךָ חָבֵר, וֶהֱוֵי דָן אֶת כָּל הָאָדָם לְכַף זְכוּת.

[ז] נִתַּאי הָאַרְבֵּלִי אוֹמֵר: הַרְחֵק מִשָּׁכֵן רָע, וְאַל תִּתְחַבֵּר לָרָשָׁע, וְאַל תִּתְיָאֵשׁ מִן הַפֻּרְעָנוּת.

[ח] יְהוּדָה בֶּן טַבַּאי וְשִׁמְעוֹן בֶּן שָׁטַח קִבְּלוּ מֵהֶם. יְהוּדָה בֶּן טַבַּאי אוֹמֵר: אַל תַּעַשׂ עַצְמְךָ כְּעוֹרְכֵי הַדַּיָּנִין; וּכְשֶׁיִּהְיוּ בַעֲלֵי הַדִּין עוֹמְדִים לְפָנֶיךָ, יִהְיוּ בְעֵינֶיךָ כִּרְשָׁעִים; וּכְשֶׁנִּפְטָרִים מִלְּפָנֶיךָ, יִהְיוּ בְעֵינֶיךָ כְּזַכָּאִין, כְּשֶׁקִּבְּלוּ עֲלֵיהֶם אֶת הַדִּין.

[ט] שִׁמְעוֹן בֶּן שָׁטַח אוֹמֵר: הֱוֵי מַרְבֶּה לַחֲקוֹר אֶת הָעֵדִים; וֶהֱוֵי זָהִיר בִּדְבָרֶיךָ, שֶׁמָּא מִתּוֹכָם יִלְמְדוּ לְשַׁקֵּר.

[י] שְׁמַעְיָה וְאַבְטַלְיוֹן קִבְּלוּ מֵהֶם. שְׁמַעְיָה אוֹמֵר: אֱהַב אֶת הַמְּלָאכָה, וּשְׂנָא אֶת הָרַבָּנוּת, וְאַל תִּתְוַדַּע לָרָשׁוּת.

---

sat on a bench and his pupils sat on the ground. Thus, Yose ben Yoezer exhorts us to become loyal disciples of the sages.

5. לִרְוָחָה — *Wide.* Make your home a center of hospitality. Some render לִרְוָחָה in the sense of *relief*, meaning that anyone who needs help of any sort can be sure of getting it from you.

וְאַל תַּרְבֶּה שִׂיחָה — *And do not converse excessively.* The mishnah warns us against idle chatter and too much of it. A man who truly respects his wife will value her views and counsel and not overburden their conversation with frivolous chatter. Moreover, this sort of bantering with other women can loosen the bounds of morality and lead to sin (R' Hirsch).

גֵּיהִנֹּם — *Gehinnom.* The place where the souls of the wicked are punished.

6. עֲשֵׂה לְךָ רַב — *Accept a teacher upon yourself,* i.e., a competent mentor who can correctly transmit the tradition, and thereby avoid error. Be willing to submit to his direction, for without a mentor to respect, a person is directionless.

חָבֵר — *A friend,* with whom to jointly engage in Torah study. "Either companionship or death," said the Talmudic sage, Choni (*Taanis* 23a). Rashi suggests that our mishnah means that one should acquire *books*: they are the best companions and are essential for acquiring Torah knowledge.

7. וְאַל תִּתְיָאֵשׁ מִן הַפֻּרְעָנוּת — *And do not despair of retribution.* The doctrine of Divine Retribution — that God eventually punishes the wicked — is one of the foundations of our faith. Even though it seems slow in coming, one must remain

1 [5] *Yose ben Yochanan, leader of Jerusalem, says: Let your house be open wide; treat the poor as members of your household; and do not converse excessively with a woman. They said this even about one's own wife; surely it applies to another's wife. Consequently, the Sages said: Anyone who converses excessively with a woman causes evil to himself, neglects Torah study, and will eventually inherit Gehinnom.*

[6] *Yehoshua ben Perachyah and Nittai of Arbel received the tradition from them. Yehoshua ben Perachyah says: Accept a teacher upon yourself, acquire a friend for yourself, and judge everyone favorably.*

[7] *Nittai of Arbel says: Distance yourself from a bad neighbor; do not associate with a wicked person; and do not despair of retribution.*

[8] *Yehudah ben Tabbai and Shimon ben Shatach received the tradition from them. Yehudah ben Tabbai says: [When serving as a judge] do not act as a lawyer; when the litigants stand before you, consider them both as guilty; but when they are dismissed from you, consider them both as innocent, provided they have accepted the judgment.*

[9] *Shimon ben Shatach says: Interrogate the witnesses extensively; and be cautious with your words, lest they learn to lie.*

[10] *Shemayah and Avtalyon received the tradition from them. Shemayah says: Love work; despise lordliness; and do not become overly familiar with the government.*

confident that there will be a time of judgment; otherwise a good person may come to feel that evil and dishonesty will always be ascendant. This passage can also be interpreted: *Do not despair because of punishment:* Even though you have been punished, remain hopeful; you can repent in sincerity and be forgiven.

8. בְּעוֹרְכֵי הַדַּיָּנִין — *As a lawyer.* This is addressed to judges: In your role of impartial arbiter, do not counsel litigants how to plead their case. Even if you are convinced of an individual's righteousness, maintain your impartiality (*Rashi; R' Hirsch*).

כִּרְשָׁעִים — *As guilty.* Not that the judge assumes the litigant to be literally *guilty,* but that he must make every effort to establish the authenticity of every statement made before him. Only through rigorous probing will he ferret out the truth.

כְּזַכָּאִין — *As innocent.* Once the verdict has been accepted, even the guilty litigant is to be regarded as having pleaded and sworn truthfully according to his own interpretation of the facts. Or, he should be viewed as having repented (*R' Yonah*).

9. יִלְמְדוּ לְשַׁקֵּר — *Learn to lie.* Speak carefully to witnesses and litigants, lest the direction of your interrogation give them a hint on how to fabricate their testimony to tell you what they think you are looking for.

10. וְשִׂנָא אֶת הָרַבָּנוּת — *Despise lordliness;* i.e., do your utmost to avoid holding positions of dominance and leadership, for they shorten a man's life (*Rashi*); shun pompousness and rank.

לָרָשׁוּת — *The government,* i.e., tyrannical authorities, who merely exploit people for their own ends. Such associations cause one to neglect religion; one

א [יא] אַבְטַלְיוֹן אוֹמֵר: חֲכָמִים, הִזָּהֲרוּ בְדִבְרֵיכֶם, שֶׁמָּא תָחוּבוּ חוֹבַת גָּלוּת וְתִגְלוּ לִמְקוֹם מַיִם הָרָעִים, וְיִשְׁתּוּ הַתַּלְמִידִים הַבָּאִים אַחֲרֵיכֶם וְיָמוּתוּ, וְנִמְצָא שֵׁם שָׁמַיִם מִתְחַלֵּל.

[יב] הִלֵּל וְשַׁמַּאי קִבְּלוּ מֵהֶם. הִלֵּל אוֹמֵר: הֱוֵי מִתַּלְמִידָיו שֶׁל אַהֲרֹן, אוֹהֵב שָׁלוֹם וְרוֹדֵף שָׁלוֹם, אוֹהֵב אֶת הַבְּרִיּוֹת וּמְקָרְבָן לַתּוֹרָה.

[יג] הוּא הָיָה אוֹמֵר: נְגִיד שְׁמָא אֲבַד שְׁמֵהּ, וּדְלָא מוֹסִיף יָסֵף, וּדְלָא יָלִיף קְטָלָא חַיָּב, וּדְאִשְׁתַּמַּשׁ בְּתָגָא חֳלָף.

[יד] הוּא הָיָה אוֹמֵר: אִם אֵין אֲנִי לִי, מִי לִי? וּכְשֶׁאֲנִי לְעַצְמִי, מָה אֲנִי? וְאִם לֹא עַכְשָׁו, אֵימָתָי?

[טו] שַׁמַּאי אוֹמֵר: עֲשֵׂה תוֹרָתְךָ קֶבַע, אֱמֹר מְעַט וַעֲשֵׂה הַרְבֵּה, וֶהֱוֵי מְקַבֵּל אֶת כָּל הָאָדָם בְּסֵבֶר פָּנִים יָפוֹת.

[טז] רַבָּן גַּמְלִיאֵל הָיָה אוֹמֵר: עֲשֵׂה לְךָ רַב, וְהִסְתַּלֵּק מִן הַסָּפֵק, וְאַל תַּרְבֶּה לְעַשֵּׂר אֲמָדוֹת.

---

cannot be a servant to two masters.

11. חֲכָמִים הִזָּהֲרוּ — *Scholars, be cautious.* The mishnah speaks allegorically of the dangerous results of unclear teachings that lend themselves to misinterpretation. Do not express yourself in a way that can be misunderstood by students other than your own. You may be forced into exile where unworthy students may sin, based on a misinterpretation of your teaching. If they die as a result of their sins, God's Name will have been desecrated.

12. אַהֲרֹן — *Aaron.* In Talmudic literature Aaron is described as the great peacemaker who went to any ends to make peace between man and wife and between feuding Jews.

13. אֲבַד שְׁמֵהּ — *Loses his reputation.* Selfish ambition to attain fame often results in one losing his reputation entirely.

יָסֵף — *Decreases it,* because he eventually forgets what he has learned previously.

וּדְלָא יָלִיף קְטָלָא חַיָּב — *He who refuses to teach [Torah] deserves death.* The translation follows *Rashi.* By refusing to share his Torah knowledge with others, one demonstrates his selfishness and his lack of concern for Torah learning, the paramount *mitzvah.* R' Yonah interprets that the mishnah refers to someone who is totally ignorant of the Torah's wisdom. Since he lacks the precious teaching that is the Jew's primary distinction, of what value is his life?

וּדְאִשְׁתַּמַּשׁ בְּתָגָא חֳלָף — *And he who exploits the crown of Torah shall fade away.* This refers to one who abuses his Torah knowledge by using it as a common tool for selfish gains. *Rashi* explains that such a person forfeits reward for his Torah study in the Hereafter since he has already gained materially from it in the present.

14. This threefold dictum refers to man's spiritual goals.

אִם אֵין אֲנִי לִי — *If I am not for myself,* i.e., if I do not rouse my soul to higher things, who will rouse it? If I do not fulfill the commandments, who will fulfill them for me?

1 [11] *Avtalyon says: Scholars, be cautious with your words, for you may incur the penalty of exile and be banished to a place of evil waters [heresy]. The disciples who follow you there may drink and die, and consequently the Name of Heaven will be desecrated.*

[12] *Hillel and Shammai received the tradition from them. Hillel says: Be among the disciples of Aaron, loving peace and pursuing peace, loving people, and bringing them closer to the Torah.*

[13] *He used to say: He who seeks renown loses his reputation; he who does not increase [his Torah learning] decreases it; he who refuses to teach [Torah] deserves death; and he who exploits the crown of Torah shall fade away.*

[14] *He used to say: If I am not for myself, who will be for me? And if I am for myself, what am I? And if not now, when?*

[15] *Shammai says: Make your Torah study a fixed practice; say little and do much; and receive everyone with a cheerful face.*

[16] *Rabban Gamliel used to say: Accept a teacher upon yourself and remove yourself from uncertainty; and do not give excess tithes by estimating [instead of measuring].*

וּכְשֶׁאֲנִי לְעַצְמִי — *And if I am for myself.* Even if I make the successful effort to grow spiritually, there is still so much more for me to do; consequently, I can never be satisfied with myself. Some comment that although man must work hard to perfect himself, he must not forget that he is part of a group that both helps him and should share in his accomplishments.

15. קֶבַע — *A fixed practice.* The study of Torah must be one's main occupation, and a regular time and schedule must be set aside for it. It must not be relegated to a secondary, casual, position in man's daily life, for Torah study determines the extent to which we will understand and fulfill our duties to God. In the ultimate sense every other pursuit is superfluous. Moreover, one should set a goal for his studies to maintain the discipline.

וַעֲשֵׂה הַרְבֵּה — *And do much.* The righteous promise little but do much; the wicked make grandiose promises but do little.

16. עֲשֵׂה לְךָ רַב — *Accept a teacher upon yourself.* The same advice occurs in mishnah 6. There the reference is to a teacher of Torah study; here, to a teacher in practical matters of *halachah*, Torah Law. Alternatively, this dictum is addressed to one who is himself an authority; even he needs another authority to consult in matters of practical halachic decisions.

וְהִסְתַּלֵּק מִן הַסָּפֵק — *And remove yourself from uncertainty,* i.e., in matters pertaining to Torah law. Moreover, avoid such things which may possibly be forbidden (*Machzor Vitry*).

אֻמָּדוֹת — *Estimating* [instead of measuring]. Tithes from the harvest must be exactly one-tenth; the allocation is to be precise, not made by guesswork. *Meiri* perceives this in the broader sense as a caution against rendering halachic decisions by conjecture; one must meticulously examine the law until it is entirely clear to him, or let him consult others.

א [יז] שִׁמְעוֹן בְּנוֹ אוֹמֵר: כָּל יָמַי גָּדַלְתִּי בֵּין הַחֲכָמִים, וְלֹא מָצָאתִי לַגּוּף טוֹב אֶלָּא שְׁתִיקָה. וְלֹא הַמִּדְרָשׁ הוּא הָעִקָּר, אֶלָּא הַמַּעֲשֶׂה. וְכָל הַמַּרְבֶּה דְבָרִים מֵבִיא חֵטְא.

[יח] רַבָּן שִׁמְעוֹן בֶּן גַּמְלִיאֵל אוֹמֵר: עַל שְׁלֹשָׁה דְבָרִים הָעוֹלָם קַיָּם — עַל הַדִּין וְעַל הָאֱמֶת וְעַל הַשָּׁלוֹם, שֶׁנֶּאֱמַר: "אֱמֶת וּמִשְׁפַּט שָׁלוֹם שִׁפְטוּ בְּשַׁעֲרֵיכֶם."

❈ ❈ ❈

רַבִּי חֲנַנְיָא בֶּן עֲקַשְׁיָא אוֹמֵר: רָצָה הַקָּדוֹשׁ בָּרוּךְ הוּא לְזַכּוֹת אֶת יִשְׂרָאֵל, לְפִיכָךְ הִרְבָּה לָהֶם תּוֹרָה וּמִצְוֹת, שֶׁנֶּאֱמַר: "יְהוָה חָפֵץ לְמַעַן צִדְקוֹ, יַגְדִּיל תּוֹרָה וְיַאְדִּיר."

❈ פרק שני ❈

ב כָּל יִשְׂרָאֵל יֵשׁ לָהֶם חֵלֶק לָעוֹלָם הַבָּא, שֶׁנֶּאֱמַר: "וְעַמֵּךְ כֻּלָּם צַדִּיקִים, לְעוֹלָם יִירְשׁוּ אָרֶץ, נֵצֶר מַטָּעַי, מַעֲשֵׂה יָדַי לְהִתְפָּאֵר."

❈ ❈ ❈

[א] רַבִּי אוֹמֵר: אֵיזוֹ הִיא דֶרֶךְ יְשָׁרָה שֶׁיָּבֹר לוֹ הָאָדָם? כָּל שֶׁהִיא תִפְאֶרֶת לְעֹשֶׂיהָ וְתִפְאֶרֶת לוֹ מִן הָאָדָם. וֶהֱוֵי זָהִיר בְּמִצְוָה קַלָּה כְּבַחֲמוּרָה, שֶׁאֵין אַתָּה יוֹדֵעַ מַתַּן שְׂכָרָן שֶׁל מִצְוֹת. וֶהֱוֵי מְחַשֵּׁב הֶפְסֵד מִצְוָה כְּנֶגֶד שְׂכָרָהּ, וּשְׂכַר עֲבֵרָה כְּנֶגֶד הֶפְסֵדָהּ. הִסְתַּכֵּל בִּשְׁלֹשָׁה דְבָרִים, וְאֵין אַתָּה בָא לִידֵי עֲבֵרָה; דַּע מַה לְּמַעְלָה מִמְּךָ — עַיִן רוֹאָה, וְאֹזֶן שׁוֹמַעַת, וְכָל מַעֲשֶׂיךָ בַּסֵּפֶר נִכְתָּבִים.

17. אֶלָּא הַמַּעֲשֶׂה — *But practice.* Though Torah study is paramount in importance beyond all other pursuits, it is the *performance* of the Torah's commandments for which man is rewarded. One must study with the intention of putting his knowledge into practice. Judaism is not a theology; it is a system of laws. The Torah's primary purpose is to regulate conduct.

18. הָעוֹלָם קַיָּם — *The world endures.* This is different from the maxim in mishnah 2. There the Sages speak of the initial act of Creation, and the three things for which the world was created; here the reference is to the spiritual forces by which the social order is held together and civilization sustained.

רַבִּי חֲנַנְיָא בֶּן עֲקַשְׁיָא — *Rabbi Chanania ben Akashia.* This excerpt is from the last mishnah in Tractate *Makkos.* The Talmud teaches that the Rabbis' *Kaddish* (p. 64) is recited only after the public study of *Aggadah.* For this reason a standard portion of the Talmud was chosen for recitation after every public study session. Although *Pirkei Avos* is Aggadic material, the universal custom of reciting this passage is maintained. The message of this excerpt is

1 [17] *Shimon his son says: All my days I have been raised among the Sages and I found nothing better for oneself than silence; not study, but practice is the main thing; and one who talks excessively brings on sin.*

[18] *Rabban Shimon ben Gamliel says: The world endures on three things — justice, truth, and peace, as it is said: "Truth and the verdict of peace are you to adjudicate in your gates."* (Zechariah 8:16).

❈ ❈ ❈

*Rabbi Chanania ben Akashia says: The Holy One, Blessed is He, wished to confer merit upon Israel; therefore He gave them Torah and mitzvos in abundance, as it is said: "H*ASHEM *desired, for the sake of its [Israel's] righteousness, that the Torah be made great and glorious."* (Isaiah 42:21).

2 ⊰§{ CHAPTER TWO }§⊱

All Israel has a share in the World to Come, as it is said: "And your people are all righteous; they shall inherit the land forever; they are the branch of My planting, My handiwork, in which to take pride" (Isaiah 60:21).

❈ ❈ ❈

[1] **רַבִּי** *Rebbi says: Which is the proper path that a man should choose for himself? Whatever is a credit to himself and earns him the esteem of fellow men. Be as scrupulous in performing a "minor" mitzvah as in a "major" one, for you do not know the reward given for the respective mitzvos. Calculate the cost of a mitzvah against its reward, and the reward of a sin against its cost. Consider three things and you will not come into the grip of sin: Know what is above you — a watchful Eye, an attentive Ear, and all your deeds are recorded in a Book.*

---

the reason it was chosen. Torah study and *mitzvah* performance are a Divinely conferred privilege.

הַרְבָּה — *Gave ... in abundance.* That is, by giving Israel the opportunity of performing so many commandments, God graciously provided them with the means of acquiring abundant merit.

CHAPTER TWO

1. רַבִּי — *Rebbi.* This refers to R' Yehudah HaNassi ("the Prince") (135-219 C.E.), redactor of the Mishnah, who was reverently referred to as *Rebbi*, teacher par excellence, and *Rabbeinu HaKadosh*, our Holy Teacher.

שֶׁאֵין אַתָּה יוֹדֵעַ מַתַּן שְׂכָרָן — *For you do not know the reward given.* God did not reveal the specific rewards for performance of the respective commandments lest everyone strive to observe only those that will earn him a greater reward.

וֶהֱוֵי מְחַשֵּׁב — *Calculate the cost.* Disregard the cost in time or money in fulfilling a *mitzvah*. Likewise, do not be misled by the pleasure or profit of a sin. Instead, calculate the eternal reward for a *mitzvah* against the temporary loss it may cause, and the eternal cost of a sin against the temporary benefit it may bring.

הִסְתַּכֵּל בִּשְׁלֹשָׁה דְבָרִים — *Consider three things.* Consider three aspects of *what is above you* and you will avoid sin. The three aspects are: (a) Man's deeds are

ב [ב] רַבָּן גַּמְלִיאֵל בְּנוֹ שֶׁל רַבִּי יְהוּדָה הַנָּשִׂיא אוֹמֵר: יָפֶה תַלְמוּד תּוֹרָה עִם דֶּרֶךְ אֶרֶץ, שֶׁיְּגִיעַת שְׁנֵיהֶם מְשַׁכַּחַת עָוֹן. וְכָל תּוֹרָה שֶׁאֵין עִמָּהּ מְלָאכָה, סוֹפָהּ בְּטֵלָה וְגוֹרֶרֶת עָוֹן. וְכָל הָעוֹסְקִים עִם הַצִּבּוּר, יִהְיוּ עוֹסְקִים עִמָּהֶם לְשֵׁם שָׁמַיִם, שֶׁזְּכוּת אֲבוֹתָם מְסַיַּעְתָּם, וְצִדְקָתָם עוֹמֶדֶת לָעַד. וְאַתֶּם, מַעֲלֶה אֲנִי עֲלֵיכֶם שָׂכָר הַרְבֵּה כְּאִלּוּ עֲשִׂיתֶם.

[ג] הֱווּ זְהִירִין בָּרָשׁוּת, שֶׁאֵין מְקָרְבִין לוֹ לְאָדָם אֶלָּא לְצוֹרֶךְ עַצְמָן; נִרְאִין כְּאוֹהֲבִין בִּשְׁעַת הֲנָאָתָן, וְאֵין עוֹמְדִין לוֹ לְאָדָם בִּשְׁעַת דָּחֳקוֹ.

[ד] הוּא הָיָה אוֹמֵר: עֲשֵׂה רְצוֹנוֹ כִּרְצוֹנֶךָ, כְּדֵי שֶׁיַּעֲשֶׂה רְצוֹנְךָ כִּרְצוֹנוֹ. בַּטֵּל רְצוֹנְךָ מִפְּנֵי רְצוֹנוֹ, כְּדֵי שֶׁיְּבַטֵּל רְצוֹן אֲחֵרִים מִפְּנֵי רְצוֹנֶךָ.

[ה] הִלֵּל אוֹמֵר: אַל תִּפְרוֹשׁ מִן הַצִּבּוּר, וְאַל תַּאֲמִין בְּעַצְמְךָ עַד יוֹם מוֹתְךָ, וְאַל תָּדִין אֶת חֲבֵרְךָ עַד שֶׁתַּגִּיעַ לִמְקוֹמוֹ, וְאַל תֹּאמַר דָּבָר שֶׁאִי אֶפְשָׁר לִשְׁמוֹעַ, שֶׁסּוֹפוֹ לְהִשָּׁמַע. וְאַל תֹּאמַר לִכְשֶׁאֶפָּנֶה אֶשְׁנֶה, שֶׁמָּא לֹא תִפָּנֶה.

[ו] הוּא הָיָה אוֹמֵר: אֵין בּוּר יְרֵא חֵטְא, וְלֹא עַם הָאָרֶץ חָסִיד, וְלֹא הַבַּיְשָׁן לָמֵד, וְלֹא הַקַּפְּדָן מְלַמֵּד, וְלֹא כָּל הַמַּרְבֶּה

observed; (b) his words are heard; (c) he cannot escape the consequences of his behavior because everything he does and says is indelibly recorded.

2. עִם דֶּרֶךְ אֶרֶץ — *With an occupation.* The ideal for spiritual reflection is a synthesis of diligent Torah study combined with an honest occupation for support. If a man's day is thereby filled, idleness that leads to sin is avoided. Others render דֶּרֶךְ אֶרֶץ in the familiar sense of *proper social conduct* which, combined with Torah study, is a deterrent to sin.

סוֹפָהּ בְּטֵלָה וְגוֹרֶרֶת עָוֹן — *Will cease in the end, and leads to sin.* Without a means of support, a scholar will not be able to continue his studies, and the press of his needs may lead him to dishonesty.

מַעֲלֶה אֲנִי עֲלֵיכֶם — *I [God] will bestow upon you.* Although your success was due in great measure to the ancestral merit of the community you serve, God will reward your unselfish efforts as if you alone were responsible for your accomplishments.

3. בָּרָשׁוּת — *Of rulers.* Although servants of the community must often deal with the government, they should always be vigilant, for the interests of rulers and those of the community may not coincide.

4. עֲשֵׂה רְצוֹנוֹ כִּרְצוֹנֶךָ — *Treat His will as if it were your own will.* Devote as much time and money to *mitzvos* as to your own desires. In return, God will help you beyond all expectations.

5. אַל תִּפְרוֹשׁ מִן הַצִּבּוּר — *Do not separate yourself from the community.* Share its woes and do nothing to undermine its solidarity.

2 [2] *Rabban Gamliel, the son of Rabbi Yehudah HaNassi, says: Torah study is good together with an occupation, for the exertion of them both makes sin forgotten. All Torah study that is not joined with work will cease in the end, and leads to sin. All who exert themselves for the community should exert themselves for the sake of Heaven, for then the merit of the community's forefathers aids them and their righteousness endures forever. Nevertheless, as for you, I [God] will bestow upon you as great a reward as if you had accomplished it on your own.*

[3] *Beware of rulers, for they befriend someone only for their own benefit; they act friendly when it benefits them, but they do not stand by someone in his time of need.*

[4] *He used to say: Treat His will as if it were your own will, so that He will treat your will as if it were His will. Nullify your will before His will, so that He will nullify the will of others before your will.*

[5] *Hillel says: Do not separate yourself from the community; do not believe in yourself until the day you die; do not judge your fellow until you have reached his place; do not say what cannot be easily understood on the ground that it will be understood eventually; and do not say, "When I am free I will study," for perhaps you will not become free.*

[6] *He used to say: A boor cannot be fearful of sin; an unlearned person cannot be scrupulously pious; the bashful person cannot learn, and the quick, impatient person cannot teach;* anyone excessively occupied in business cannot become a scholar; *and in a*

וְאַל תַּאֲמִין בְּעַצְמְךָ — *Do not believe in yourself.* Piety must never be taken for granted. One must remain on guard against sin throughout his life.

עַד שֶׁתַּגִּיעַ לִמְקוֹמוֹ — *Until you have reached his place.* You never know how you would react if you were in the same predicament. You cannot condemn a person who succumbed to temptation unless you have overcome a similar challenge.

וְאַל תֹּאמַר — *(And) do not say.* One's words must be immediately understandable to the listener. Unless a teacher makes himself clear, his doctrine may be misinterpreted and cause harm.

לִכְשֶׁאֶפָּנֶה — *When I am free.* The Evil Inclination always urges you to wait for a more opportune time. Rather, every available moment, no matter how short and seemingly insignificant, should be utilized for Torah study.

6. בּוּר — *Boor.* An uncultivated and uncivilized person has little regard for right and wrong.

עַם הָאָרֶץ — *Unlearned person,* i.e., unlearned in Torah. The term חָסִיד, *scrupulously pious,* refers to someone who goes further than the minimum requirements of the law. An unlearned person remains blind to the requirements of the law, and so cannot be pious.

הַקַּפְּדָן — *The quick, impatient person.* Because he will not tolerate questions, students will be afraid to seek clarification.

הַמַּרְבֶּה בִסְחוֹרָה — *Excessively occupied in business.* Though it is meritorious to

בְּסַחְוֹרָה מַחְכִּימִים, וּבְמָקוֹם שֶׁאֵין אֲנָשִׁים הִשְׁתַּדֵּל לִהְיוֹת אִישׁ.

[ז] אַף הוּא רָאָה גֻלְגֹּלֶת אַחַת שֶׁצָּפָה עַל פְּנֵי הַמָּיִם. אָמַר לָהּ: "עַל דַּאֲטֵפְתְּ אַטְפוּךְ, וְסוֹף מְטַיְּפַיִךְ יְטוּפוּן."

[ח] הוּא הָיָה אוֹמֵר: מַרְבֶּה בָשָׂר, מַרְבֶּה רִמָּה; מַרְבֶּה נְכָסִים, מַרְבֶּה דְאָגָה; מַרְבֶּה נָשִׁים, מַרְבֶּה כְשָׁפִים; מַרְבֶּה שְׁפָחוֹת, מַרְבֶּה זִמָּה; מַרְבֶּה עֲבָדִים, מַרְבֶּה גָזֵל. מַרְבֶּה תוֹרָה, מַרְבֶּה חַיִּים; מַרְבֶּה יְשִׁיבָה, מַרְבֶּה חָכְמָה; מַרְבֶּה עֵצָה, מַרְבֶּה תְבוּנָה; מַרְבֶּה צְדָקָה, מַרְבֶּה שָׁלוֹם. קָנָה שֵׁם טוֹב, קָנָה לְעַצְמוֹ; קָנָה לוֹ דִבְרֵי תוֹרָה, קָנָה לוֹ חַיֵּי הָעוֹלָם הַבָּא.

[ט] רַבָּן יוֹחָנָן בֶּן זַכַּאי קִבֵּל מֵהִלֵּל וּמִשַּׁמַּאי. הוּא הָיָה אוֹמֵר: אִם לָמַדְתָּ תּוֹרָה הַרְבֵּה, אַל תַּחֲזִיק טוֹבָה לְעַצְמְךָ, כִּי לְכָךְ נוֹצָרְתָּ.

[י] חֲמִשָּׁה תַלְמִידִים הָיוּ לוֹ לְרַבָּן יוֹחָנָן בֶּן זַכַּאי, וְאֵלוּ הֵן: רַבִּי אֱלִיעֶזֶר בֶּן הוֹרְקְנוֹס, רַבִּי יְהוֹשֻׁעַ בֶּן חֲנַנְיָא, רַבִּי יוֹסֵי הַכֹּהֵן, רַבִּי שִׁמְעוֹן בֶּן נְתַנְאֵל, וְרַבִּי אֶלְעָזָר בֶּן עֲרָךְ.

[יא] הוּא הָיָה מוֹנֶה שְׁבָחָן: רַבִּי אֱלִיעֶזֶר בֶּן הוֹרְקְנוֹס, בּוֹר סוּד שֶׁאֵינוֹ מְאַבֵּד טִפָּה; רַבִּי יְהוֹשֻׁעַ בֶּן חֲנַנְיָא, אַשְׁרֵי יוֹלַדְתּוֹ; רַבִּי יוֹסֵי הַכֹּהֵן, חָסִיד; רַבִּי שִׁמְעוֹן בֶּן נְתַנְאֵל, יְרֵא חֵטְא; וְרַבִּי אֶלְעָזָר בֶּן עֲרָךְ, כְּמַעְיָן הַמִּתְגַּבֵּר.

[יב] הוּא הָיָה אוֹמֵר: אִם יִהְיוּ כָּל חַכְמֵי יִשְׂרָאֵל בְּכַף מֹאזְנַיִם, וֶאֱלִיעֶזֶר בֶּן הוֹרְקְנוֹס בְּכַף שְׁנִיָּה, מַכְרִיעַ אֶת כֻּלָּם. אַבָּא

combine intensive Torah study with an occupation [mishnah 2 above], one who is excessively absorbed in business will relegate Torah to a subordinate position and never become wise.

שֶׁאֵין אֲנָשִׁים — *Where there are no leaders* [lit., *men*]. When there is no one to accept communal and spiritual responsibility and provide leadership, we are bidden to rise to the occasion and fill the role. The implication, however, is that where there are competent "men," we are to stand aside and devote ourselves to the study of Torah (*Rashi*). According to *R' Yonah*, the "leader" is someone to direct us upon the proper path of God's service. In the absence of such a person, we must strive to improve ourselves.

7. עַל דַּאֲטֵפְתְּ — *Because you drowned others.* Moved by this sight of a floating skull that had been deprived of proper burial (*Tiferes Yisrael*), Hillel remarked aloud about the justice of Divine retribution: God punishes man "measure for measure." Nothing man experiences in life is without reason. The commentators agree that Hillel meant his statement only in *general* terms, but he did not mean that every corpse was that of a murderer. Many victims had never

פרקי אבות / פרק ב [18]

2 *place where there are no leaders, strive to be a leader.*

[7] *He also saw a skull floating on the water; he said to it: "Because you drowned others, they drowned you; and those who drowned you will be drowned eventually."*

[8] *He used to say: The more flesh, the more worms; the more possessions, the more worry; the more wives, the more witchcraft; the more maidservants, the more lewdness; the more manservants, the more thievery. [However,] the more Torah, the more life; the more study, the more wisdom; the more counsel, the more understanding; the more charity, the more peace. One who has gained a good reputation has gained it for his own benefit; one who has gained himself Torah knowledge has gained himself the life of the World to Come.*

[9] *Rabban Yochanan ben Zakkai received the tradition from Hillel and Shammai. He used to say: If you have studied much Torah, do not take credit for yourself, because that is what you were created to do.*

[10] *Rabban Yochanan ben Zakkai had five [primary] disciples. They were: Rabbi Eliezer ben Hyrkanos, Rabbi Yehoshua ben Chanania, Rabbi Yose the Kohen, Rabbi Shimon ben Nesanel, and Rabbi Elazar ben Arach.*

[11] *He used to enumerate their praises: Rabbi Eliezer ben Hyrkanos is like a cemented cistern that loses not a drop; Rabbi Yehoshua ben Chanania, praiseworthy is she who bore him; Rabbi Yose the Kohen is a scrupulously pious person; Rabbi Shimon ben Nesanel fears sin; and Rabbi Elazar ben Arach is like a spring flowing stronger and stronger.*

[12] *He used to say: If all the Sages of Israel were on one pan of a balance-scale, and Eliezer ben Hyrkanos were on the other, he*

committed such a crime, but Hillel's point is that there is always justice in God's scheme.

יְטוּפוּן — *Will be drowned.* Those who drowned you were also not guiltless, and therefore God used them as His tools to perpetrate this illegal act (מִגַּלְגְּלִין חוֹב עַל יְדֵי חַיָּב). Accordingly, they will also be punished.

8. The dicta in this mishnah denounce excess and overindulgence in life; only extensive Torah study and piety bring beneficial results. While other things might *seem* desirable to many, they can have an adverse affect on those who pursue them.

רִמָּה — *Worms.* One's corpulent body becomes food for maggots in the grave; a denunciation of gluttony.

כְּשָׁפִים — *Witchcraft.* The condemnation of polygamy focuses upon the jealousy between rival wives. They may resort to anything — even witchcraft — to gain their husband's affection.

9. כִּי לְכָךְ נוֹצָרְתָּ — *Because that is what you were created to do.* Intelligence was given you only for the purpose of acquiring knowledge, and you may not become arrogant for having utilized this knowledge, any more than a bird may for utilizing its wings to fly (*Mesillas Yesharim*).

11. שֶׁאֵינוֹ מְאַבֵּד טִפָּה — *That loses not a drop.* He retained everything he ever learned.

ב שָׁאוּל אוֹמֵר מִשְּׁמוֹ: אִם יִהְיוּ כָּל חַכְמֵי יִשְׂרָאֵל בְּכַף מֹאזְנַיִם, וְרַבִּי אֱלִיעֶזֶר בֶּן הָרְקָנוֹס אַף עִמָּהֶם, וְרַבִּי אֶלְעָזָר בֶּן עֲרָךְ בְּכַף שְׁנִיָּה, מַכְרִיעַ אֶת כֻּלָּם.

[יג] אָמַר לָהֶם: צְאוּ וּרְאוּ אֵיזוֹ הִיא דֶרֶךְ טוֹבָה שֶׁיִּדְבַּק בָּהּ הָאָדָם. רַבִּי אֱלִיעֶזֶר אוֹמֵר: עַיִן טוֹבָה. רַבִּי יְהוֹשֻׁעַ אוֹמֵר: חָבֵר טוֹב. רַבִּי יוֹסֵי אוֹמֵר: שָׁכֵן טוֹב. רַבִּי שִׁמְעוֹן אוֹמֵר: הָרוֹאֶה אֶת הַנּוֹלָד. רַבִּי אֶלְעָזָר אוֹמֵר: לֵב טוֹב. אָמַר לָהֶם: רוֹאֶה אֲנִי אֶת דִּבְרֵי אֶלְעָזָר בֶּן עֲרָךְ מִדִּבְרֵיכֶם, שֶׁבִּכְלַל דְּבָרָיו דִּבְרֵיכֶם.

[יד] אָמַר לָהֶם: צְאוּ וּרְאוּ אֵיזוֹ הִיא דֶרֶךְ רָעָה שֶׁיִּתְרַחֵק מִמֶּנָּה הָאָדָם. רַבִּי אֱלִיעֶזֶר אוֹמֵר: עַיִן רָעָה. רַבִּי יְהוֹשֻׁעַ אוֹמֵר: חָבֵר רָע. רַבִּי יוֹסֵי אוֹמֵר: שָׁכֵן רָע. רַבִּי שִׁמְעוֹן אוֹמֵר: הַלֹּוֶה וְאֵינוֹ מְשַׁלֵּם. אֶחָד הַלֹּוֶה מִן הָאָדָם כְּלֹוֶה מִן הַמָּקוֹם, שֶׁנֶּאֱמַר: „לֹוֶה רָשָׁע וְלֹא יְשַׁלֵּם, וְצַדִּיק חוֹנֵן וְנוֹתֵן." רַבִּי אֶלְעָזָר אוֹמֵר: לֵב רָע. אָמַר לָהֶם: רוֹאֶה אֲנִי אֶת דִּבְרֵי אֶלְעָזָר בֶּן עֲרָךְ מִדִּבְרֵיכֶם, שֶׁבִּכְלַל דְּבָרָיו דִּבְרֵיכֶם.

[טו] הֵם אָמְרוּ שְׁלֹשָׁה דְבָרִים. רַבִּי אֱלִיעֶזֶר אוֹמֵר: יְהִי כְבוֹד חֲבֵרְךָ חָבִיב עָלֶיךָ כְּשֶׁלָּךְ, וְאַל תְּהִי נוֹחַ לִכְעוֹס; וְשׁוּב יוֹם אֶחָד לִפְנֵי מִיתָתְךָ; וֶהֱוֵי מִתְחַמֵּם כְּנֶגֶד אוּרָן שֶׁל חֲכָמִים, וֶהֱוֵי זָהִיר בְּגַחַלְתָּן שֶׁלֹּא תִכָּוֶה — שֶׁנְּשִׁיכָתָן נְשִׁיכַת שׁוּעָל, וַעֲקִיצָתָן עֲקִיצַת עַקְרָב, וּלְחִישָׁתָן לְחִישַׁת שָׂרָף, וְכָל דִּבְרֵיהֶם כְּגַחֲלֵי אֵשׁ.

[טז] רַבִּי יְהוֹשֻׁעַ אוֹמֵר: עַיִן הָרָע, וְיֵצֶר הָרָע, וְשִׂנְאַת הַבְּרִיּוֹת מוֹצִיאִין אֶת הָאָדָם מִן הָעוֹלָם.

---

13. אָמַר לָהֶם — *He said to them.* Rabban Yochanan to his disciples.

שֶׁיִּדְבַּק — *Should cling.* In order to live meritoriously and inherit the life of the World to Come.

עַיִן טוֹבָה — *A good eye.* An attitude of tolerance and benevolence toward others.

חָבֵר טוֹב — *A good friend.* Both *being* one and *acquiring* one. (See note to 1:6.)

שָׁכֵן טוֹב — *A good neighbor,* even more influential than a *good friend.* Because of his close proximity, one has more opportunity to learn from his good behavior.

הָרוֹאֶה אֶת הַנּוֹלָד — *One who considers the outcome of a deed.* This refers to one who foresees the consequences of his actions.

לֵב טוֹב — *A good heart.* The *heart* symbolizes the emotion and desire that are at the root of every endeavor, aspiration, spiritual tendency, and achieve-

2 would outweigh them all. Abba Shaul said in his name: If all the Sages of Israel, with even Rabbi Eliezer ben Hyrkanos among them, were on one pan of the balance-scale, and Rabbi Elazar ben Arach were on the other, he would outweigh them all.

[13] He said to them: Go out and discern which is the proper way to which a man should cling. Rabbi Eliezer says: A good eye. Rabbi Yehoshua says: A good friend. Rabbi Yose says: A good neighbor. Rabbi Shimon says: One who considers the outcome of a deed. Rabbi Elazar says: A good heart. He [Rabban Yochanan ben Zakkai] said to them: I prefer the words of Elazar ben Arach to your words, for your words are included in his words.

[14] He said to them: Go out and discern which is the evil path from which a man should distance himself. Rabbi Eliezer says: An evil eye. Rabbi Yehoshua says: A wicked friend. Rabbi Yose says: A wicked neighbor. Rabbi Shimon says: One who borrows and does not repay; one who borrows from man is like one who borrows from the Omnipresent, as it is said: "The wicked one borrows and does not repay, but the Righteous One is gracious and gives" (Psalms 37:21). Rabbi Elazar said: A wicked heart. He [Rabban Yochanan ben Zakkai] said to them: I prefer the words of Elazar ben Arach to your words, for your words are included in his words.

[15] They each said three things. Rabbi Eliezer says: (a) Let your fellow's honor be as dear to you as your own and do not anger easily; (b) repent one day before your death; and (c) warm yourself by the fire of the sages, but beware of their glowing coal lest you be burnt — for their bite is the bite of a fox, their sting is the sting of a scorpion, their hiss is the hiss of a serpent, and all their words are like fiery coals.

[16] Rabbi Yehoshua says: (a) An evil eye, (b) the evil inclination, and (c) hatred of other people remove a person from the world.

---

ment. Thus the term לֵב טוֹב includes all the stimuli that lead people toward goodness, provided they obey the dictates of their noble instincts.

14. עַיִן רָעָה — *An evil eye*, i.e., greed, ill will; the opposite of a "good eye" in the previous mishnah.

כְּלֹוֶה מִן הַמָּקוֹם — *Is like one who borrows from the Omnipresent.* When a borrower betrays the lender who trusted him, God Himself — צַדִּיק, the *Righteous One* — recompenses the lender. Thus, it is as if the borrower took the money from God.

15. הֵם אָמְרוּ שְׁלֹשָׁה דְבָרִים — *They each* [i.e., each one of the five disciples mentioned in mishnah 10] *said three things* on the subject of ethics.

וְשׁוּב יוֹם אֶחָד לִפְנֵי מִיתָתְךָ — *Repent one day before your death.* R' Eliezer's disciples asked, "But does one know the day of his death?" He explained, "Let him repent each day lest he die on the morrow."

וֶהֱוֵי מִתְחַמֵּם כְּנֶגֶד אוּרָן שֶׁל חֲכָמִים — *Warm yourself by the fire of the sages.* One should keep in close contact with Torah scholars to learn from their ways.

ב [יז] רַבִּי יוֹסֵי אוֹמֵר: יְהִי מָמוֹן חֲבֵרְךָ חָבִיב עָלֶיךָ כְּשֶׁלָּךְ; וְהַתְקֵן עַצְמְךָ לִלְמוֹד תּוֹרָה, שֶׁאֵינָהּ יְרֻשָּׁה לָךְ; וְכָל מַעֲשֶׂיךָ יִהְיוּ לְשֵׁם שָׁמָיִם.

[יח] רַבִּי שִׁמְעוֹן אוֹמֵר: הֱוֵי זָהִיר בִּקְרִיאַת שְׁמַע וּבִתְפִלָּה; וּכְשֶׁאַתָּה מִתְפַּלֵּל, אַל תַּעַשׂ תְּפִלָּתְךָ קֶבַע, אֶלָּא רַחֲמִים וְתַחֲנוּנִים לִפְנֵי הַמָּקוֹם, שֶׁנֶּאֱמַר: ,,כִּי חַנּוּן וְרַחוּם הוּא אֶרֶךְ אַפַּיִם וְרַב חֶסֶד וְנִחָם עַל הָרָעָה"; וְאַל תְּהִי רָשָׁע בִּפְנֵי עַצְמֶךָ.

[יט] רַבִּי אֶלְעָזָר אוֹמֵר: הֱוֵי שָׁקוּד לִלְמוֹד תּוֹרָה, וְדַע מַה שֶׁתָּשִׁיב לְאֶפִּיקוֹרוֹס; וְדַע לִפְנֵי מִי אַתָּה עָמֵל; וְנֶאֱמָן הוּא בַּעַל מְלַאכְתְּךָ, שֶׁיְּשַׁלֵּם לְךָ שְׂכַר פְּעֻלָּתֶךָ.

[כ] רַבִּי טַרְפוֹן אוֹמֵר: הַיּוֹם קָצֵר, וְהַמְּלָאכָה מְרֻבָּה, וְהַפּוֹעֲלִים עֲצֵלִים, וְהַשָּׂכָר הַרְבֵּה, וּבַעַל הַבַּיִת דּוֹחֵק.

[כא] הוּא הָיָה אוֹמֵר: לֹא עָלֶיךָ הַמְּלָאכָה לִגְמוֹר, וְלֹא אַתָּה בֶן חוֹרִין לְהִבָּטֵל מִמֶּנָּה. אִם לָמַדְתָּ תּוֹרָה הַרְבֵּה, נוֹתְנִים לְךָ שָׂכָר הַרְבֵּה, וְנֶאֱמָן הוּא בַּעַל מְלַאכְתְּךָ, שֶׁיְּשַׁלֵּם לְךָ שְׂכַר פְּעֻלָּתֶךָ. וְדַע שֶׁמַּתַּן שְׂכָרָן שֶׁל צַדִּיקִים לֶעָתִיד לָבֹא.

❈ ❈ ❈

רַבִּי חֲנַנְיָא בֶּן עֲקַשְׁיָא אוֹמֵר: רָצָה הַקָּדוֹשׁ בָּרוּךְ הוּא לְזַכּוֹת אֶת יִשְׂרָאֵל, לְפִיכָךְ הִרְבָּה לָהֶם תּוֹרָה וּמִצְוֹת, שֶׁנֶּאֱמַר: ,,יהוה חָפֵץ לְמַעַן צִדְקוֹ, יַגְדִּיל תּוֹרָה וְיַאְדִּיר."

However, if he becomes too close, to the point where he becomes casual and disrespectful, they may burn him with a stinging admonition.

17. שֶׁאֵינָהּ יְרֻשָּׁה לָךְ — *For it is not yours by inheritance.* One cannot attain scholarship on the merit of his father's studies; everyone must acquire knowledge by personal effort.

לְשֵׁם שָׁמַיִם — *For the sake of Heaven.* For the sake of God, i.e., with pure purpose and good intentions. Every action, however mundane and secular, should be consecrated to the service of God, and not merely done for personal benefit. For example, one should always intend that even his eating, sleeping, etc., are for the purpose of strengthening his body for serving God.

18. וְאַל תְּהִי רָשָׁע בִּפְנֵי עַצְמֶךָ — *And do not judge yourself to be a wicked person.* This teaches the obligation for self-esteem. Do not consider yourself so beyond help that you lose hope for Divine mercy, and as a result you do not pray properly and repent. If you give up on yourself, you will fall.

19. וְדַע מַה שֶׁתָּשִׁיב לְאֶפִּיקוֹרוֹס — *And know what to answer a heretic.* Immerse yourself in Torah knowledge and laws so you can defend the Torah against malicious opponents.

2 [17] *Rabbi Yose says: (a) Let your fellow's money be as dear to you as your own; (b) apply yourself to study Torah, for it is not yours by inheritance; and (c) let all your deeds be for the sake of Heaven.*

[18] *Rabbi Shimon says: (a) Be meticulous in reading the Shema and in prayer; (b) when you pray, do not make your prayer a set routine, but rather [beg for] compassion and supplication before the Omnipresent, as it is said: "For He is gracious and compassionate, slow to anger, abounding in kindness, and relentful of punishment" (Joel 2:13); and (c) do not judge yourself to be a wicked person.*

[19] *Rabbi Elazar says: (a) Be diligent in the study of Torah and know what to answer a heretic; (b) know before Whom you toil; and (c) know that your Employer can be relied upon to pay you the wage of your labor.*

[20] *Rabbi Tarfon says: The day is short, the task is abundant, the laborers are lazy, the wage is great, and the Master of the house is insistent.*

[21] *He used to say: You are not required to complete the task, yet you are not free to withdraw from it. If you have studied much Torah, they will give you great reward; and your Employer can be relied upon to pay you the wage for your labor, but be aware that the reward of the righteous will be given in the World to Come.*

❧ ❧ ❧

*Rabbi Chanania ben Akashia says: The Holy One, Blessed is He, wished to confer merit upon Israel; therefore He gave them Torah and mitzvos in abundance, as it is said: "*Hashem *desired, for the sake of its [Israel's] righteousness, that the Torah be made great and glorious" (Isaiah 42:12).*

---

20. הַיּוֹם — *The day*, i.e., man's life span.

וְהַמְּלָאכָה — *[And] the task*, i.e., of utilizing one's life in acquiring Torah knowledge and serving God. Therefore time is too precious to waste.

וּבַעַל הַבַּיִת — *And the Master of the house*, i.e., God — Master of the universe.

21. הַמְּלָאכָה — *The task.* See comment to mishnah 20. Do not be discouraged at the magnitude of what remains to be accomplished; God does not expect one individual to complete it alone. Man is required only to do as much as his abilities allow.

‡§ פרק שלישי ‡§

כָּל יִשְׂרָאֵל יֵשׁ לָהֶם חֵלֶק לָעוֹלָם הַבָּא, שֶׁנֶּאֱמַר: "וְעַמֵּךְ כֻּלָּם צַדִּיקִים, לְעוֹלָם יִירְשׁוּ אָרֶץ, נֵצֶר מַטָּעַי, מַעֲשֵׂה יָדַי לְהִתְפָּאֵר".

[א] **עֲקַבְיָא** בֶּן מַהֲלַלְאֵל אוֹמֵר: הִסְתַּכֵּל בִּשְׁלֹשָׁה דְבָרִים וְאֵין אַתָּה בָא לִידֵי עֲבֵרָה: דַּע מֵאַיִן בָּאתָ, וּלְאָן אַתָּה הוֹלֵךְ, וְלִפְנֵי מִי אַתָּה עָתִיד לִתֵּן דִּין וְחֶשְׁבּוֹן. מֵאַיִן בָּאתָ? מִטִּפָּה סְרוּחָה. וּלְאָן אַתָּה הוֹלֵךְ? לִמְקוֹם עָפָר, רִמָּה וְתוֹלֵעָה. וְלִפְנֵי מִי אַתָּה עָתִיד לִתֵּן דִּין וְחֶשְׁבּוֹן? לִפְנֵי מֶלֶךְ מַלְכֵי הַמְּלָכִים, הַקָּדוֹשׁ בָּרוּךְ הוּא.

[ב] רַבִּי חֲנִינָא סְגַן הַכֹּהֲנִים אוֹמֵר: הֱוֵי מִתְפַּלֵּל בִּשְׁלוֹמָהּ שֶׁל מַלְכוּת, שֶׁאִלְמָלֵא מוֹרָאָהּ, אִישׁ אֶת רֵעֵהוּ חַיִּים בְּלָעוֹ.

[ג] רַבִּי חֲנִינָא בֶּן תְּרַדְיוֹן אוֹמֵר: שְׁנַיִם שֶׁיּוֹשְׁבִין וְאֵין בֵּינֵיהֶם דִּבְרֵי תוֹרָה, הֲרֵי זֶה מוֹשַׁב לֵצִים, שֶׁנֶּאֱמַר: "וּבְמוֹשַׁב לֵצִים לֹא יָשָׁב". אֲבָל שְׁנַיִם שֶׁיּוֹשְׁבִין וְיֵשׁ בֵּינֵיהֶם דִּבְרֵי תוֹרָה, שְׁכִינָה שְׁרוּיָה בֵּינֵיהֶם, שֶׁנֶּאֱמַר: "אָז נִדְבְּרוּ יִרְאֵי יהוה אִישׁ אֶל רֵעֵהוּ, וַיַּקְשֵׁב יהוה וַיִּשְׁמָע, וַיִּכָּתֵב סֵפֶר זִכָּרוֹן לְפָנָיו, לְיִרְאֵי יהוה וּלְחֹשְׁבֵי שְׁמוֹ". אֵין לִי אֶלָּא שְׁנַיִם; מִנַּיִן שֶׁאֲפִילוּ אֶחָד שֶׁיּוֹשֵׁב וְעוֹסֵק בַּתּוֹרָה, שֶׁהַקָּדוֹשׁ בָּרוּךְ הוּא קוֹבֵעַ לוֹ שָׂכָר? שֶׁנֶּאֱמַר: "יֵשֵׁב בָּדָד וְיִדֹּם, כִּי נָטַל עָלָיו".

[ד] רַבִּי שִׁמְעוֹן אוֹמֵר: שְׁלֹשָׁה שֶׁאָכְלוּ עַל שֻׁלְחָן אֶחָד וְלֹא אָמְרוּ עָלָיו דִּבְרֵי תוֹרָה, כְּאִלּוּ אָכְלוּ מִזִּבְחֵי מֵתִים, שֶׁנֶּאֱמַר: "כִּי כָּל שֻׁלְחָנוֹת מָלְאוּ קִיא צֹאָה, בְּלִי מָקוֹם"; אֲבָל שְׁלֹשָׁה

CHAPTER THREE

1. וְאֵין אַתָּה בָּא לִידֵי עֲבֵרָה — *And you will not come into the grip of sin.* Reflection upon one's origins will induce humility, the lack of which results in pride and sinfulness. Similarly, man's contemplation of his physical end will help him put his sensual lusts into perspective, for it is only man's spiritual and moral elements that will remain eternal. And to constantly recall the day of reckoning will inspire man with the true fear of God.

2. מַלְכוּת — *Government.* The government maintains social order and peace, and by instilling fear of the law it prevents anarchy and wanton crime from destroying the fabric of society.

3. The main subject of the rest of this chapter is the importance of Torah study and, conversely, the grave seriousness of failure to study and value it properly.

הֲרֵי זֶה מוֹשַׁב לֵצִים — *It is a session of scorners.* They are scorners not in the

CHAPTER THREE

3

All Israel has a share in the World to Come, as it is said: "And your people are all righteous; they shall inherit the land forever; they are the branch of My planting, My handiwork, in which to take pride" (Isaiah 60:21).

❦ ❦ ❦

[1] **עֲקַבְיָא** Akavia ben Mahalalel says: Consider three things and you will not come into the grip of sin: Know whence you came, whither you go, and before Whom you will give justification and reckoning. "Whence you came?" — from a putrid drop; "whither you go?" — to a place of dust, worms, and maggots; "and before Whom you will give justification and reckoning?" — before the King Who reigns over kings, the Holy One, Blessed is He.

[2] Rabbi Chanina, the deputy Kohen Gadol [High Priest], says: Pray for the welfare of the government, because if people did not fear it, a person would swallow his fellow alive.

[3] Rabbi Chanina ben Tradyon says: If two sit together and there are no words of Torah between them, it is a session of scorners, as it is said: "In the session of scorners he does not sit" (Psalms 1:1). But if two sit together and words of Torah are between them, the Divine Presence rests between them, as it is said: "Then those who fear HASHEM spoke to each other, and HASHEM listened and heard, and a book of remembrance was written before Him for those who fear HASHEM and give thought to His Name" (Malachi 3:16). From this verse we would know this only about two people; how do we know that if even one person sits and occupies himself with Torah the Holy One, Blessed is He, determines a reward for him? For it is said: "Let one sit in solitude and be still, for he will have received [a reward] for it" (Lamentations 3:28).

[4] Rabbi Shimon says: If three have eaten at the same table and have not spoken words of Torah there, it is as if they have eaten of offerings to dead idols, as it is said: "For all tables are full of vomit and filth, without the Omnipresent" (Isaiah 28:8). But if three have

---

usual sense of someone who slanders or harms someone, but in the sense that they imply contempt for the Torah, by not utilizing an opportunity to study (R' Yonah). As the commentators explain, we know that these *scorners* are people who do not study because the very next verse (Psalms 1:2) says that the opposite of the scorner is one whose *desire* is in *the Torah of* HASHEM.

אָז נִדְבְּרוּ יִרְאֵי ה׳ אִישׁ אֶל רֵעֵהוּ — *Then those who fear* HASHEM *spoke to each other.* The verse implies that only two people

are speaking together [*to each other*], but because they speak of matters that express their fear of God, their deed is so precious that God Himself listens and records their words as an eternal keepsake for Himself.

יֵשֵׁב בָּדָד וְיִדֹּם — *Let one sit in solitude and be still.* One who studies alone tends to do so quietly. Nevertheless, even a solitary individual studying Torah is valuable in God's eyes.

4. שְׁלֹשָׁה שֶׁאָכְלוּ — *If three have eaten.* By taking in spiritual nourishment while

ג. שֶׁאָכְלוּ עַל שֻׁלְחָן אֶחָד וְאָמְרוּ עָלָיו דִּבְרֵי תוֹרָה, כְּאִלּוּ אָכְלוּ מִשֻּׁלְחָנוֹ שֶׁל מָקוֹם, שֶׁנֶּאֱמַר: "וַיְדַבֵּר אֵלַי, 'זֶה הַשֻּׁלְחָן אֲשֶׁר לִפְנֵי יהוה'".

[ה] רַבִּי חֲנִינָא בֶּן חֲכִינַאי אוֹמֵר: הַנֵּעוֹר בַּלַּיְלָה, וְהַמְהַלֵּךְ בַּדֶּרֶךְ יְחִידִי, וּמְפַנֶּה לִבּוֹ לְבַטָּלָה — הֲרֵי זֶה מִתְחַיֵּב בְּנַפְשׁוֹ.

[ו] רַבִּי נְחוּנְיָא בֶּן הַקָּנָה אוֹמֵר: כָּל הַמְקַבֵּל עָלָיו עֹל תּוֹרָה, מַעֲבִירִין מִמֶּנּוּ עֹל מַלְכוּת וְעֹל דֶּרֶךְ אֶרֶץ; וְכָל הַפּוֹרֵק מִמֶּנּוּ עֹל תּוֹרָה, נוֹתְנִין עָלָיו עֹל מַלְכוּת וְעֹל דֶּרֶךְ אֶרֶץ.

[ז] רַבִּי חֲלַפְתָּא בֶּן דּוֹסָא אִישׁ כְּפַר חֲנַנְיָא אוֹמֵר: עֲשָׂרָה שֶׁיּוֹשְׁבִין וְעוֹסְקִין בַּתּוֹרָה, שְׁכִינָה שְׁרוּיָה בֵּינֵיהֶם, שֶׁנֶּאֱמַר: "אֱלֹהִים נִצָּב בַּעֲדַת אֵל". וּמִנַּיִן אֲפִלּוּ חֲמִשָּׁה? שֶׁנֶּאֱמַר: "וַאֲגֻדָּתוֹ עַל אֶרֶץ יְסָדָהּ". וּמִנַּיִן אֲפִלּוּ שְׁלֹשָׁה? שֶׁנֶּאֱמַר: "בְּקֶרֶב אֱלֹהִים יִשְׁפֹּט". וּמִנַּיִן אֲפִלּוּ שְׁנַיִם? שֶׁנֶּאֱמַר: "אָז נִדְבְּרוּ יִרְאֵי יהוה אִישׁ אֶל רֵעֵהוּ וַיַּקְשֵׁב יהוה וַיִּשְׁמָע". וּמִנַּיִן אֲפִלּוּ אֶחָד? שֶׁנֶּאֱמַר: "בְּכָל הַמָּקוֹם אֲשֶׁר אַזְכִּיר אֶת שְׁמִי, אָבוֹא אֵלֶיךָ וּבֵרַכְתִּיךָ".

he eats, a person consecrates his table. Then it may be truly said that he ate at God's table. This obligation of Torah study may be fulfilled by the recitation of the Grace After Meals since it contains Scriptural passages, although it is meritorious to engage in additional Torah discourses during meals.

The mishnah deduces from the verse in *Isaiah* that three people shared the meal, because the prophet had been discussing the activities of three people: a scholar, a prophet, and a *Kohen*. Had there been only two people, perhaps they would not have been judged so harshly, but in a group of three at least one of them should have reminded his colleagues to stop their idle chatter (*Tos. Yom Tov*).

"וַיְדַבֵּר אֵלַי, 'זֶה הַשֻּׁלְחָן...'" — "*And he said to me, 'This is the table ....'*" Although the table of the verse refers to the Temple Altar that an angel had been showing to the prophet Ezekiel, the Sages understand it also to be an allusion to the table of human beings. Thus, it teaches that we can give our dining table a sanctity that makes it like a sacred vessel that is *before* HASHEM.

5. הַנֵּעוֹר בַּלַּיְלָה — *One who stays awake at night.* This person wastes his nights on idle thoughts rather than utilizing them to study Torah, for which the quiet of night is particularly suited. Not only does he fail to utilize the time best suited for spiritual elevation, he also spurns the Torah's protective powers against the dangers of the night.

וְהַמְהַלֵּךְ בַּדֶּרֶךְ יְחִידִי — *Or who travels alone on the road.* He is unaccompanied by a companion with whom to study Torah, and at the same time is exposed to the perils of the way because he lacks the protection afforded by Torah study.

3 *eaten at the same table and have spoken words of Torah there, it is as if they have eaten from the table of the Omnipresent, as it is said: "And he said to me, 'This is the table that is before HASHEM.'" (Ezekiel 41:22).*

[5] *Rabbi Chanina ben Chachinai says: One who stays awake at night or who travels alone on the road, but turns his heart to idleness — indeed, he bears guilt for his soul.*

[6] *Rabbi Nechunia ben Hakanah says: If someone takes upon himself the yoke of Torah — the yoke of government and the yoke of worldly responsibilities are removed from him. But if someone throws off the yoke of Torah from himself — the yoke of government and the yoke of worldly responsibilities are placed upon him.*

[7] *Rabbi Chalafta ben Dosa of Kfar Chanania says: If ten people sit together and engage in Torah study, the Divine Presence rests among them, as it is said: "God stands in the assembly of God"(Psalms 82:1). How do we know this even of five? For it is said: "He has established His bundle upon earth" (Amos 9:6). How do we know this even of three? For it is said: "In the midst of judges He shall judge" (Psalms 82:1). How do we know this even of two? For it is said: "Then those who fear HASHEM spoke to each other, and HASHEM listened and heard" (Malachi 3:16). How do we know this even of one? For it is said: "In every place where I cause My Name to be mentioned, I will come to you and bless you" (Exodus 20:21).*

By not utilizing those solitary times to engage in study, he exposes himself to danger — and has only himself to blame.

6. מֵעָבִירִין מִמֶּנּוּ — *Are removed from him.* One who devotes himself primarily to the "burden" of Torah acquires endurance, serenity, and contentment. In effect, he frees himself from being adversely affected by the rigors and anxieties of earthly cares. He does not feel pressured by the burdens of the government and of everyday secular living. The converse is also true. The *Chofetz Chaim* used to counsel that everyone must have cares in his life; we have the choice of being burdened with spiritual strivings or with mundane cares that drain us but do not offer blessings.

7. Rabbi Chalafta teaches that God's Presence joins those who study Torah. His concluding words are that even a solitary student merits this blessing — why then need he enumerate groups of ten, five, three, and two? The more people join in performing a good deed, the greater its cumulative value; a multitude studying Torah together is better than a group of unrelated individuals (R' Yonah; cf. *Berachos* 6a).

בַּעֲדַת אֵל — *In the assembly of God.* The Sages (*Berachos* 21b) derive from Scripture that the term עֵדָה, assembly, refers to at least ten people.

חֲמִשָּׁה ... אֲגֻדָּתוֹ — *Five ... His bundle.* The word אֲגֻדָּה usually refers to a quantity of sheaves or other articles that can be grasped in the five fingers of one hand. The word is also used for the hand or any other group of five (*Rambam*).

שְׁלֹשָׁה ... אֱלֹהִים — *Three ... judges.* The minimum number of judges that can constitute a *beis din* is three.

ג [ח] רַבִּי אֶלְעָזָר אִישׁ בַּרְתּוֹתָא אוֹמֵר: תֶּן לוֹ מִשֶּׁלּוֹ, שֶׁאַתָּה וְשֶׁלְּךָ שֶׁלּוֹ; וְכֵן בְּדָוִד הוּא אוֹמֵר: „כִּי מִמְּךָ הַכֹּל, וּמִיָּדְךָ נָתַנּוּ לָךְ".

[ט] רַבִּי יַעֲקֹב אוֹמֵר: הַמְהַלֵּךְ בַּדֶּרֶךְ וְשׁוֹנֶה, וּמַפְסִיק מִמִּשְׁנָתוֹ, וְאוֹמֵר: „מַה נָּאֶה אִילָן זֶה! וּמַה נָּאֶה נִיר זֶה"! — מַעֲלֶה עָלָיו הַכָּתוּב כְּאִלּוּ מִתְחַיֵּב בְּנַפְשׁוֹ.

[י] רַבִּי דּוֹסְתַּאי בַּר יַנַּאי מִשּׁוּם רַבִּי מֵאִיר אוֹמֵר: כָּל הַשּׁוֹכֵחַ דָּבָר אֶחָד מִמִּשְׁנָתוֹ, מַעֲלֶה עָלָיו הַכָּתוּב כְּאִלּוּ מִתְחַיֵּב בְּנַפְשׁוֹ, שֶׁנֶּאֱמַר: „רַק הִשָּׁמֶר לְךָ, וּשְׁמֹר נַפְשְׁךָ מְאֹד, פֶּן תִּשְׁכַּח אֶת הַדְּבָרִים אֲשֶׁר רָאוּ עֵינֶיךָ". יָכוֹל אֲפִלּוּ תָּקְפָה עָלָיו מִשְׁנָתוֹ? תַּלְמוּד לוֹמַר: „וּפֶן יָסוּרוּ מִלְּבָבְךָ כֹּל יְמֵי חַיֶּיךָ"; הָא אֵינוֹ מִתְחַיֵּב בְּנַפְשׁוֹ עַד שֶׁיֵּשֵׁב וִיסִירֵם מִלִּבּוֹ.

[יא] רַבִּי חֲנִינָא בֶּן דּוֹסָא אוֹמֵר: כָּל שֶׁיִּרְאַת חֶטְאוֹ קוֹדֶמֶת לְחָכְמָתוֹ, חָכְמָתוֹ מִתְקַיֶּמֶת; וְכֹל שֶׁחָכְמָתוֹ קוֹדֶמֶת לְיִרְאַת חֶטְאוֹ, אֵין חָכְמָתוֹ מִתְקַיֶּמֶת.

[יב] הוּא הָיָה אוֹמֵר: כֹּל שֶׁמַּעֲשָׂיו מְרֻבִּין מֵחָכְמָתוֹ, חָכְמָתוֹ מִתְקַיֶּמֶת; וְכֹל שֶׁחָכְמָתוֹ מְרֻבָּה מִמַּעֲשָׂיו, אֵין חָכְמָתוֹ מִתְקַיֶּמֶת.

[יג] הוּא הָיָה אוֹמֵר: כֹּל שֶׁרוּחַ הַבְּרִיּוֹת נוֹחָה הֵימֶנּוּ, רוּחַ הַמָּקוֹם נוֹחָה הֵימֶנּוּ; וְכֹל שֶׁאֵין רוּחַ הַבְּרִיּוֹת נוֹחָה הֵימֶנּוּ, אֵין רוּחַ הַמָּקוֹם נוֹחָה הֵימֶנּוּ.

[יד] רַבִּי דּוֹסָא בֶּן הָרְכִּינָס אוֹמֵר: שֵׁנָה שֶׁל שַׁחֲרִית, וְיַיִן שֶׁל צָהֳרַיִם, וְשִׂיחַת הַיְלָדִים, וִישִׁיבַת בָּתֵּי כְנֵסִיּוֹת שֶׁל עַמֵּי הָאָרֶץ — מוֹצִיאִין אֶת הָאָדָם מִן הָעוֹלָם.

---

8. תֶּן לוֹ מִשֶּׁלּוֹ — *Give Him from His Own.* An inspiring exhortation to be generous in dispensing charity. Man should withhold neither himself nor his wealth from the wishes of Heaven. All that he is and has belongs to God, and he should be ready to dedicate all his faculties in fulfillment of God's will. (For R' Elazar's own lavish generosity in alms-giving, see *Taanis* 24a.)

9. וּמַפְסִיק מִמִּשְׁנָתוֹ — *But interrupts his review.* It is not the expression of praise for the beauty of God's creation that is condemned here, but the interruption of one's studies. The point is that during Torah study, one's attention should not be diverted to common things, however noble. Moreover, one who journeys is exposed to harm, and if one interrupts his study of Torah, which is his safe-

3 [8] *Rabbi Elazar of Bartosa says: Give Him from His Own, for you and your possessions are His. And so has David said, "For everything is from You, and from Your Own we have given You" (I Chronicles 29:14).*

[9] *Rabbi Yaakov says: One who walks on the road while reviewing [a Torah lesson] but interrupts his review and exclaims, "How beautiful is this tree! How beautiful is this plowed field!" — Scripture considers it as if he bears guilt for his soul.*

[10] *Rabbi Dostai bar Yannai says in the name of Rabbi Meir: Whoever forgets anything of his Torah learning, Scripture considers it as if he bears guilt for his soul, for it is said: "But beware and guard your soul exceedingly lest you forget the things your eyes have seen" (Deuteronomy 4:9). Does this apply even if [he forgot because] his studies were too difficult for him? [This is not so, for] Scripture says, "And lest they be removed from your heart all the days of your life" (ibid.). Thus, one does not bear guilt for his soul unless he sits [idly] and [through lack of concentration and review] removes them from his consciousness.*

[11] *Rabbi Chanina ben Dosa says: Anyone whose fear of sin takes priority over his wisdom, his wisdom will endure; but anyone whose wisdom takes priority over his fear of sin, his wisdom will not endure.*

[12] *He used to say: Anyone whose good deeds exceed his wisdom, his wisdom will endure; but anyone whose wisdom exceeds his good deeds, his wisdom will not endure.*

[13] *He used to say: If the spirit of one's fellows is pleased with him, the spirit of the Omnipresent is pleased with him; but if the spirit of one's fellows is not pleased with him, the spirit of the Omnipresent is not pleased with him.*

[14] *Rabbi Dosa ben Harkinas says: Late morning sleep, midday wine, children's chatter, and sitting in the assemblies of the ignorant remove a man from the world.*

guard, he incurs danger.

10. כָּל הַשּׁוֹכֵחַ — *Whoever forgets,* i.e., due to negligence, laziness, or indifference. One is obligated to review his studies regularly to minimize the natural process of forgetfulness. The mishnah condemns one who fails to make every attempt to retain what he has learned. This is the implication of וּפֶן יָסוּרוּ מִלְּבָבְךָ, *and lest they be removed from your heart*; i.e., you had mastered this knowledge, but allowed yourself to forget it.

11-12. Man's acquired wisdom can endure only if it is secondary to his fear of God; if wisdom is made an end unto itself, it lacks a moral foundation and it must fail. Similarly, one's performance of the Torah must exceed his wisdom; wisdom without observance cannot endure; see 1:17.

13. כָּל שֶׁרוּחַ הַבְּרִיּוֹת נוֹחָה הֵימֶנּוּ — *If the spirit of one's fellows is pleased with him.* If someone behaves in a courteous, ethical, trustworthy manner, he sanctifies God's Name by gaining the affection of his peers.

14. שֵׁנָה שֶׁל שַׁחֲרִית — *Late morning sleep.*

ג [טו] רַבִּי אֱלְעָזָר הַמּוֹדָעִי אוֹמֵר: הַמְחַלֵּל אֶת הַקֳּדָשִׁים, וְהַמְבַזֶּה אֶת הַמּוֹעֲדוֹת, וְהַמַּלְבִּין פְּנֵי חֲבֵרוֹ בָּרַבִּים, וְהַמֵּפֵר בְּרִיתוֹ שֶׁל אַבְרָהָם אָבִינוּ, וְהַמְגַלֶּה פָנִים בַּתּוֹרָה שֶׁלֹּא כַהֲלָכָה, אַף עַל פִּי שֶׁיֵּשׁ בְּיָדוֹ תּוֹרָה וּמַעֲשִׂים טוֹבִים — אֵין לוֹ חֵלֶק לָעוֹלָם הַבָּא.

[טז] רַבִּי יִשְׁמָעֵאל אוֹמֵר: הֱוֵי קַל לְרֹאשׁ, וְנוֹחַ לְתִשְׁחֹרֶת, וֶהֱוֵי מְקַבֵּל אֶת כָּל הָאָדָם בְּשִׂמְחָה.

[יז] רַבִּי עֲקִיבָא אוֹמֵר: שְׂחוֹק וְקַלּוּת רֹאשׁ מַרְגִּילִין אֶת הָאָדָם לְעֶרְוָה. מָסֹרֶת סְיָג לַתּוֹרָה; מַעַשְׂרוֹת סְיָג לָעֹשֶׁר; נְדָרִים סְיָג לַפְּרִישׁוּת; סְיָג לַחָכְמָה שְׁתִיקָה.

[יח] הוּא הָיָה אוֹמֵר: חָבִיב אָדָם שֶׁנִּבְרָא בְצֶלֶם; חִבָּה יְתֵרָה נוֹדַעַת לוֹ שֶׁנִּבְרָא בְצֶלֶם, שֶׁנֶּאֱמַר: "כִּי בְּצֶלֶם אֱלֹהִים עָשָׂה אֶת הָאָדָם". חֲבִיבִין יִשְׂרָאֵל, שֶׁנִּקְרְאוּ בָנִים לַמָּקוֹם; חִבָּה יְתֵרָה נוֹדַעַת לָהֶם שֶׁנִּקְרְאוּ בָנִים לַמָּקוֹם, שֶׁנֶּאֱמַר: "בָּנִים אַתֶּם לַיהוה אֱלֹהֵיכֶם". חֲבִיבִין יִשְׂרָאֵל, שֶׁנִּתַּן לָהֶם כְּלִי חֶמְדָּה; חִבָּה יְתֵרָה נוֹדַעַת לָהֶם, שֶׁנִּתַּן לָהֶם כְּלִי חֶמְדָּה, שֶׁנֶּאֱמַר: "כִּי לֶקַח טוֹב נָתַתִּי לָכֶם, תּוֹרָתִי אַל תַּעֲזֹבוּ".

[יט] הַכֹּל צָפוּי, וְהָרְשׁוּת נְתוּנָה. וּבְטוֹב הָעוֹלָם נָדוֹן, וְהַכֹּל לְפִי רֹב הַמַּעֲשֶׂה.

[כ] הוּא הָיָה אוֹמֵר: הַכֹּל נָתוּן בָּעֵרָבוֹן, וּמְצוּדָה פְרוּסָה עַל כָּל הַחַיִּים. הַחֲנוּת פְּתוּחָה, וְהַחֶנְוָנִי מַקִּיף, וְהַפִּנְקָס פָּתוּחַ, וְהַיָּד כּוֹתֶבֶת, וְכָל הָרוֹצֶה לִלְווֹת יָבֹא וְיִלְוֶה, וְהַגַּבָּאִים מַחֲזִירִין

Beyond the time prescribed for the saying of the *Shema* and of prayer. The idle pursuits mentioned by the mishnah represent a squandering of time that should be used to carry out one's mission on earth.

15. וְהַמֵּפֵר בְּרִיתוֹ — *Who nullifies the covenant.* By refusing to be circumcised, or by surgically concealing his circumcision.

אֵין לוֹ חֵלֶק לָעוֹלָם הַבָּא — *He has no share in the World to Come*, because he demonstrates contempt for sanctity.

17. מַעַשְׂרוֹת סְיָג לָעֹשֶׁר — *Tithes are a protective fence for wealth.* The discipline of contributing tithes to charity makes the owner cognizant of the true Owner of all wealth; thereby it makes him worthy of even greater fortune. On the words עַשֵּׂר תְּעַשֵּׂר, literally, *you are to give tithes* (*Deut.* 14:22), the sages homiletically expound עַשֵּׂר בִּשְׁבִיל שֶׁתִּתְעַשֵּׁר, *Give tithes so you will become wealthy* (*Taanis* 9a).

שְׁתִיקָה — *Silence.* Not total silence, but moderation in ordinary conversation. See 1:17. By doing so, a person avoids

3 [15] *Rabbi Elazar the Moda'ite says: One who desecrates sacred things, who disgraces the Festivals, who humiliates his fellow in public, who nullifies the covenant of our forefather Abraham, or who perverts the Torah contrary to the halachah — though he may have Torah and good deeds, he has no share in the World to Come.*

[16] *Rabbi Yishmael says: Be yielding to a superior, pleasant to the young, and receive every person cheerfully.*

[17] *Rabbi Akiva said: Mockery and levity accustom a man to immorality. The transmitted Oral Torah is a protective fence around the Torah; tithes are a protective fence for wealth; vows are a protective fence for abstinence; a protective fence for wisdom is silence.*

[18] *He used to say: Beloved is man, for he was created in God's image; it is indicative of a greater love that it was made known to him that he was created in God's image, as it is said: "For in the image of God He made man" (Genesis 9:6) Beloved are the people Israel, for they are described as children of the Omnipresent; it is indicative of a greater love that it was made known to them that they are described as children of the Omnipresent, as it is said: "You are children to* HASHEM, *Your God" (Deuteronomy 14:1) Beloved are the people Israel, for a cherished utensil was given to them; it is indicative of a greater love that it was made known to them that they were given a cherished utensil, as it is said: "For I have given you a good teaching; do not forsake My Torah" (Proverbs 4:2)*

[19] *Everything is foreseen, yet the freedom of choice is given. The world is judged with goodness, and everything depends on the abundance of good deeds.*

[20] *He used to say: Everything is given on collateral and a net is spread over all the living. The shop is open; the Merchant extends credit; the ledger is open; the hand writes; and whoever wishes to borrow, let him come and borrow. The collectors make their rounds*

being drawn into sin and controversy, which would detract from his pursuit of Torah wisdom.

18. חִבָּה יְתֵרָה — *A greater love.* By letting Israel know its privileged status, God not only gave it cause for pride, but let it know what its spiritual goals should be.

19. הַכֹּל צָפוּי, וְהָרְשׁוּת נְתוּנָה — *Everything is foreseen, yet the freedom of choice is given.* This is a fundamental concept of Divine Providence. Although God foresees the path a man will adopt, this in no way restricts man's complete freedom of choice. Nothing is imposed upon man, and God's foreknowledge and man's free will are not contradictory.

וְהַכֹּל לְפִי רוֹב הַמַּעֲשֶׂה — *And everything depends on the abundance of good deeds.* Man is condemned or acquitted according to the *preponderance* of his good or bad deeds. Alternatively, one should accustom himself to repeating good deeds over and over again.

20. הַכֹּל נָתוּן בָּעֵרָבוֹן — *Everything is given on collateral.* God's conduct of the world is likened to a business: He grants man

[31] **PIRKEI AVOS** / CHAPTER 3

ג. תָּדִיר בְּכָל יוֹם וְנִפְרָעִין מִן הָאָדָם, מִדַּעְתּוֹ וְשֶׁלֹּא מִדַּעְתּוֹ, וְיֵשׁ לָהֶם עַל מַה שֶּׁיִּסְתְּמְכוּ. וְהַדִּין דִּין אֱמֶת, וְהַכֹּל מְתֻקָּן לַסְּעוּדָה.

[כא] רַבִּי אֶלְעָזָר בֶּן עֲזַרְיָה אוֹמֵר: אִם אֵין תּוֹרָה, אֵין דֶּרֶךְ אֶרֶץ; אִם אֵין דֶּרֶךְ אֶרֶץ, אֵין תּוֹרָה. אִם אֵין חָכְמָה, אֵין יִרְאָה; אִם אֵין יִרְאָה, אֵין חָכְמָה. אִם אֵין דַּעַת, אֵין בִּינָה; אִם אֵין בִּינָה, אֵין דַּעַת. אִם אֵין קֶמַח, אֵין תּוֹרָה; אִם אֵין תּוֹרָה, אֵין קֶמַח.

[כב] הוּא הָיָה אוֹמֵר: כֹּל שֶׁחָכְמָתוֹ מְרֻבָּה מִמַּעֲשָׂיו, לְמָה הוּא דוֹמֶה? לְאִילָן שֶׁעֲנָפָיו מְרֻבִּין וְשָׁרָשָׁיו מוּעָטִין, וְהָרוּחַ בָּאָה וְעוֹקַרְתּוֹ וְהוֹפַכְתּוֹ עַל פָּנָיו, שֶׁנֶּאֱמַר: „וְהָיָה כְּעַרְעָר בָּעֲרָבָה, וְלֹא יִרְאֶה כִּי יָבוֹא טוֹב, וְשָׁכַן חֲרֵרִים בַּמִּדְבָּר, אֶרֶץ מְלֵחָה וְלֹא תֵשֵׁב". אֲבָל כֹּל שֶׁמַּעֲשָׂיו מְרֻבִּין מֵחָכְמָתוֹ, לְמָה הוּא דוֹמֶה? לְאִילָן שֶׁעֲנָפָיו מוּעָטִין וְשָׁרָשָׁיו מְרֻבִּין, שֶׁאֲפִילוּ כָּל הָרוּחוֹת שֶׁבָּעוֹלָם בָּאוֹת וְנוֹשְׁבוֹת בּוֹ, אֵין מְזִיזִין אוֹתוֹ מִמְּקוֹמוֹ, שֶׁנֶּאֱמַר: „וְהָיָה כְּעֵץ שָׁתוּל עַל מַיִם, וְעַל יוּבַל יְשַׁלַּח שָׁרָשָׁיו, וְלֹא יִרְאֶה כִּי יָבוֹא חוֹם, וְהָיָה עָלֵהוּ רַעֲנָן, וּבִשְׁנַת בַּצֹּרֶת לֹא יִדְאָג, וְלֹא יָמִישׁ מֵעֲשׂוֹת פֶּרִי".

[כג] רַבִּי אֶלְעָזָר בֶּן חִסְמָא אוֹמֵר: קִנִּין וּפִתְחֵי נִדָּה הֵן הֵן גּוּפֵי הֲלָכוֹת; תְּקוּפוֹת וְגִמַטְרִיָּאוֹת — פַּרְפְּרָאוֹת לַחָכְמָה.

❧ ❧ ❧

רַבִּי חֲנַנְיָא בֶּן עֲקַשְׁיָא אוֹמֵר: רָצָה הַקָּדוֹשׁ בָּרוּךְ הוּא לְזַכּוֹת אֶת יִשְׂרָאֵל, לְפִיכָךְ הִרְבָּה לָהֶם תּוֹרָה וּמִצְוֹת, שֶׁנֶּאֱמַר: „יהוה חָפֵץ לְמַעַן צִדְקוֹ, יַגְדִּיל תּוֹרָה וְיַאְדִּיר".

---

the goodness of this world, freedom, and opportunities on the "pledge" that he will utilize them properly. No unpaid debt — however long-term — is ever canceled, and no one can evade his responsibilities.

לַסְּעוּדָה — *For the [final festive] banquet.* To be enjoyed by the righteous in the World to Come.

21. אֵין דֶּרֶךְ אֶרֶץ — *There is no worldly occupation.* See note 2:2. The laws of the Torah regulate commerce and business ethics; therefore, without Torah knowledge and fidelity to its laws, one's business practices may well be improper.

דַּעַת... בִּינָה — *Knowledge ... understanding.* Both are necessary. Mere accumulation of knowledge is sterile without the reasoning and understanding which enable it to be integrated and applied.

אִם אֵין קֶמַח — *If there is no flour,* i.e., sustenance. The body must be nourished

3 *constantly, every day, and collect payment from the person whether he realizes it or not. They have proof to rely upon; the judgment is a truthful judgment; and everything is prepared for the [final festive] banquet.*

[21] *Rabbi Elazar ben Azariah says: If there is no Torah, there is no worldly occupation; if there is no worldly occupation, there is no Torah. If there is no wisdom, there is no fear of God; if there is no fear of God, there is no wisdom. If there is no knowledge, there is no understanding; if there is no understanding, there is no knowledge. If there is no flour, there is no Torah; if there is no Torah, there is no flour.*

[22] *He used to say: Anyone whose wisdom exceeds his good deeds, to what is he likened? — to a tree whose branches are numerous but whose roots are few; then the wind comes and uproots it and turns it upside down; as it is said: "And he shall be like an isolated tree in an arid land and shall not see when good comes; he shall dwell on parched soil in the wilderness, on a salted land, uninhabited" (Jeremiah 17:6). But one whose good deeds exceed his wisdom, to what is he likened? — to a tree whose branches are few but whose roots are numerous; even if all the winds in the world were to come and blow against it, they could not budge it from its place; as it is said: "And he shall be like a tree planted by waters, toward the stream spreading its roots, and it shall not notice the heat's arrival, and its foliage shall be fresh; in the year of drought it shall not worry, nor shall it cease from yielding fruit" (ibid. 17:8).*

[23] *Rabbi Elazar ben Chisma said: The laws of bird-offerings, and the laws regarding the beginning of menstrual periods — these are the essential laws; astronomy and mathematics are like the seasonings of wisdom.*

❧ ❧ ❧

*Rabbi Chanania ben Akashia says: The Holy One, Blessed is He, wished to confer merit upon Israel; therefore He gave them Torah and mitzvos in abundance, as it is said: "*HASHEM *desired, for the sake of its [Israel's] righteousness, that the Torah be made great and glorious" (Isaiah 42:21).*

---

properly in order to function effectively; without nourishment, one cannot study properly. Conversely, physical nourishment — the acquisition of material things only — is not enough: Man's intellect must be nourished with Torah as well.

23. קִנִּין וּפִתְחֵי נִדָּה — *The laws of bird-offerings* [see *Leviticus* 12:8]*, and the laws regarding the beginning of menstrual periods.* These are areas of study which may appear to be an unworthy or unattractive subject for the true scholar. The mishnah therefore emphasizes that no study of Torah law is to be taken lightly — such laws are essential. Similarly, other pursuits, such as astronomy and mathematics — or, according to some, the mystical study of numerical values of Hebrew letters — are "seasonings of wisdom." These disciplines should be studied only after one has "filled his stomach" with the study of Torah and Talmud.

פרק רביעי

כָּל יִשְׂרָאֵל יֵשׁ לָהֶם חֵלֶק לָעוֹלָם הַבָּא, שֶׁנֶּאֱמַר: "וְעַמֵּךְ כֻּלָּם צַדִּיקִים, לְעוֹלָם יִירְשׁוּ אָרֶץ, נֵצֶר מַטָּעַי, מַעֲשֵׂה יָדַי לְהִתְפָּאֵר".

[א] **בֶּן זוֹמָא** אוֹמֵר: אֵיזֶהוּ חָכָם? הַלּוֹמֵד מִכָּל אָדָם, שֶׁנֶּאֱמַר: "מִכָּל מְלַמְּדַי הִשְׂכַּלְתִּי". אֵיזֶהוּ גִּבּוֹר? הַכּוֹבֵשׁ אֶת יִצְרוֹ, שֶׁנֶּאֱמַר: "טוֹב אֶרֶךְ אַפַּיִם מִגִּבּוֹר, וּמֹשֵׁל בְּרוּחוֹ מִלֹּכֵד עִיר". אֵיזֶהוּ עָשִׁיר? הַשָּׂמֵחַ בְּחֶלְקוֹ, שֶׁנֶּאֱמַר: "יְגִיעַ כַּפֶּיךָ כִּי תֹאכֵל אַשְׁרֶיךָ וְטוֹב לָךְ". "אַשְׁרֶיךָ" — בָּעוֹלָם הַזֶּה, "וְטוֹב לָךְ" — לָעוֹלָם הַבָּא. אֵיזֶהוּ מְכֻבָּד? הַמְכַבֵּד אֶת הַבְּרִיּוֹת, שֶׁנֶּאֱמַר: "כִּי מְכַבְּדַי אֲכַבֵּד, וּבֹזַי יֵקָלּוּ".

[ב] בֶּן עַזַּאי אוֹמֵר: הֱוֵי רָץ לְמִצְוָה קַלָּה, וּבוֹרֵחַ מִן הָעֲבֵרָה; שֶׁמִּצְוָה גּוֹרֶרֶת מִצְוָה, וַעֲבֵרָה גּוֹרֶרֶת עֲבֵרָה, שֶׁשְּׂכַר מִצְוָה מִצְוָה, וּשְׂכַר עֲבֵרָה עֲבֵרָה.

[ג] הוּא הָיָה אוֹמֵר: אַל תְּהִי בָז לְכָל אָדָם, וְאַל תְּהִי מַפְלִיג לְכָל דָּבָר, שֶׁאֵין לְךָ אָדָם שֶׁאֵין לוֹ שָׁעָה, וְאֵין לְךָ דָּבָר שֶׁאֵין לוֹ מָקוֹם.

[ד] רַבִּי לְוִיטַס אִישׁ יַבְנֶה אוֹמֵר: מְאֹד מְאֹד הֱוֵי שְׁפַל רוּחַ, שֶׁתִּקְוַת אֱנוֹשׁ רִמָּה.

[ה] רַבִּי יוֹחָנָן בֶּן בְּרוֹקָא אוֹמֵר: כָּל הַמְחַלֵּל שֵׁם שָׁמַיִם בַּסֵּתֶר, נִפְרָעִין מִמֶּנּוּ בַּגָּלוּי. אֶחָד שׁוֹגֵג וְאֶחָד מֵזִיד בְּחִלּוּל הַשֵּׁם.

CHAPTER FOUR

1. אֵיזֶהוּ חָכָם — *Who is wise?* Ben Zoma does not mean to say that people cannot be wise, strong, rich, happy, or honored unless they comply with his definitions. Rather, he is telling us that people are entitled to take pride in their achievements only if they are attained and exercised in accordance with the moral teachings of the Torah.

הַלּוֹמֵד מִכָּל אָדָם — *He who learns from every person.* One who truly values wisdom will seek it wherever it can be found. For a person to refuse to learn from someone because he dislikes or disapproves of that someone is to elevate his feelings — however justified — over his pursuit of knowledge.

אֵיזֶהוּ עָשִׁיר — *Who is rich?* What good is wealth if it does not provide happiness? Therefore, the truly wealthy person is the contented one.

אֵיזֶהוּ מְכֻבָּד — *Who is honored?* A person with the above virtues is truly worthy of honor whether or not his neighbors acknowledge it. But how does one gain the recognition of others as well? — by honoring *them.* If even God repays honor with honor, surely people will do the same.

4

✥ CHAPTER FOUR ✥

All Israel has a share in the World to Come, as it is said: "And your people are all righteous; they shall inherit the land forever; they are the branch of My planting, My handiwork, in which to take pride" (Isaiah 60:21).

[1] **בֶּן זוֹמָא** *Ben Zoma says: Who is wise? He who learns from every person, as it is said: "From all my teachers I grew wise" (Psalms 119:99). Who is strong? He who subdues his personal inclination, as it is said: "He who is slow to anger is better than the strong man, and a master of his passions is better than a conqueror of a city" (Proverbs 16:32). Who is rich? He who is happy with his lot, as it is said: "When you eat of the labor of your hands, you are praiseworthy and all is well with you" (Psalms 128:2). "You are praiseworthy" — in this world; "and all is well with you" — in the World to Come. Who is honored? He who honors others, as it is said: "For those who honor Me I will honor, and those who scorn Me shall be degraded"(I Samuel 2:30).*

[2] *Ben Azzai says: Run to perform even a "minor" mitzvah, and flee from sin; for one mitzvah leads to another mitzvah, and one sin leads to another sin; for the consequence of a mitzvah is a mitzvah, and the consequence of a sin is a sin.*

[3] *He used to say: Do not be scornful of any person and do not be disdainful of anything, for you have no person without his hour and no thing without its place.*

[4] *Rabbi Levitas of Yavneh says: Be exceedingly humble in spirit, for the anticipated end of mortal man is worms.*

[5] *Rabbi Yochanan ben Beroka says: Whoever desecrates the Name of Heaven in secret, they will exact punishment from him in public; unintentional or intentional, both are alike regarding desecration of the Name.*

2. שֶׁמִּצְוָה גּוֹרֶרֶת מִצְוָה — *For one mitzvah leads to another mitzvah.* When someone performs a *mitzvah* he becomes conditioned to obey God's will; conversely, each wrongful act dulls the conscience.

5. חִלּוּל הַשֵּׁם — *Desecration of the Name* involves the sort of conduct that makes onlookers think or say that people who claim to be observant Jews act in an unworthy manner. For some of the great Talmudic sages, even to take a few paces without studying Torah constituted a desecration. For ordinary people, rudeness, dishonesty, and the like would be a desecration. One who does things that bring God's Name into disrepute חִלּוּל הַשֵּׁם shows contempt for God and this is the most serious of all sins, especially because of the effect it has on others. Even an unintentional desecration is most serious, if it is the result of insufficient care or concern. Just as people cannot justify carelessness where the health and life of their loved ones are involved, so too one who is truly concerned with the honor of God will not permit an unintentional desecration to take place. Because it is so serious a sin, one who could have avoided or prevented it has no right to excuse himself

[ו] רַבִּי יִשְׁמָעֵאל בַּר רַבִּי יוֹסֵי אוֹמֵר: הַלּוֹמֵד עַל מְנָת לְלַמֵּד, מַסְפִּיקִין בְּיָדוֹ לִלְמוֹד וּלְלַמֵּד; וְהַלּוֹמֵד עַל מְנָת לַעֲשׂוֹת, מַסְפִּיקִין בְּיָדוֹ לִלְמוֹד וּלְלַמֵּד, לִשְׁמוֹר וְלַעֲשׂוֹת.

[ז] רַבִּי צָדוֹק אוֹמֵר: אַל תִּפְרוֹשׁ מִן הַצִּבּוּר; וְאַל תַּעַשׂ עַצְמְךָ כְּעוֹרְכֵי הַדַּיָּנִין; וְאַל תַּעֲשֶׂהָ עֲטָרָה לְהִתְגַּדֵּל בָּהּ, וְלֹא קַרְדֹּם לַחְפּוֹר בָּהּ. וְכָךְ הָיָה הִלֵּל אוֹמֵר: וּדְאִשְׁתַּמֵּשׁ בְּתָגָא חֲלָף. הָא לָמַדְתָּ: כָּל הַנֶּהֱנֶה מִדִּבְרֵי תוֹרָה, נוֹטֵל חַיָּיו מִן הָעוֹלָם.

[ח] רַבִּי יוֹסֵי אוֹמֵר: כָּל הַמְכַבֵּד אֶת הַתּוֹרָה, גּוּפוֹ מְכֻבָּד עַל הַבְּרִיּוֹת; וְכָל הַמְחַלֵּל אֶת הַתּוֹרָה, גּוּפוֹ מְחֻלָּל עַל הַבְּרִיּוֹת.

[ט] רַבִּי יִשְׁמָעֵאל בְּנוֹ אוֹמֵר: הַחוֹשֵׂךְ עַצְמוֹ מִן הַדִּין, פּוֹרֵק מִמֶּנּוּ אֵיבָה וְגָזֵל וּשְׁבוּעַת שָׁוְא. וְהַגַּס לִבּוֹ בְּהוֹרָאָה, שׁוֹטֶה רָשָׁע וְגַס רוּחַ.

[י] הוּא הָיָה אוֹמֵר: אַל תְּהִי דָן יְחִידִי, שֶׁאֵין דָּן יְחִידִי אֶלָּא אֶחָד. וְאַל תֹּאמַר: "קַבְּלוּ דַעְתִּי"! שֶׁהֵן רַשָּׁאִין וְלֹא אָתָּה.

[יא] רַבִּי יוֹנָתָן אוֹמֵר: כָּל הַמְקַיֵּם אֶת הַתּוֹרָה מֵעֹנִי, סוֹפוֹ לְקַיְּמָהּ מֵעֹשֶׁר; וְכָל הַמְבַטֵּל אֶת הַתּוֹרָה מֵעֹשֶׁר, סוֹפוֹ לְבַטְּלָהּ מֵעֹנִי.

[יב] רַבִּי מֵאִיר אוֹמֵר: הֱוֵי מְמַעֵט בְּעֵסֶק, וַעֲסֹק בַּתּוֹרָה; וֶהֱוֵי שְׁפַל רוּחַ בִּפְנֵי כָל אָדָם; וְאִם בָּטַלְתָּ מִן הַתּוֹרָה, יֶשׁ לְךָ בְּטֵלִים הַרְבֵּה כְּנֶגְדֶּךָ; וְאִם עָמַלְתָּ בַּתּוֹרָה, יֵשׁ לוֹ שָׂכָר הַרְבֵּה לִתֶּן לָךְ.

[יג] רַבִּי אֱלִיעֶזֶר בֶּן יַעֲקֹב אוֹמֵר: הָעוֹשֶׂה מִצְוָה אַחַת קוֹנֶה לוֹ פְּרַקְלִיט אֶחָד; וְהָעוֹבֵר עֲבֵרָה אַחַת, קוֹנֶה לוֹ קַטֵּיגוֹר

by saying it was unintended.

6. Learning is of great importance; using this knowledge to teach others is even greater, while the ultimate purpose of all study is performance.

7. אַל תִּפְרוֹשׁ ... וְאַל תַּעַשׂ — *Do not separate yourself ... do not act.* R' Tzadok apparently took these sayings of Hillel (2:5) and Yehudah ben Tabbai (1:8) as his motto.

8. וְכָל הַמְחַלֵּל אֶת הַתּוֹרָה — *And whoever disgraces the Torah,* by using it for personal gain, or by living a debased life.

9. הַחוֹשֵׂךְ עַצְמוֹ מִן הַדִּין — *One who withdraws from judgment.* If more competent judges are available, one should withdraw in their favor; otherwise, the most qualified judge has a responsibility to accept the case (R' Yonah). Rashi interprets that a judge should attempt to bring about compromises rather than render definitive judgments.

4 [6] *Rabbi Yishmael bar Rabbi Yose says:* One who studies Torah in order to teach is given the means to study and to teach; and one who studies in order to practice is given the means to study and to teach, to observe and to practice.

[7] *Rabbi Tzadok says:* Do not separate yourself from the community; [when serving as a judge] do not act as a lawyer; do not make the Torah a crown for self-glorification, nor a spade with which to dig. So too Hillel used to say: He who exploits the crown [of Torah for personal benefit] shall fade away. From this you derive that whoever seeks personal benefit from the words of Torah removes his life from the world.

[8] *Rabbi Yose says:* Whoever honors the Torah is himself honored by people; and whoever disgraces the Torah is himself disgraced by people.

[9] *Rabbi Yishmael his son says:* One who withdraws from judgment removes from himself hatred, robbery, and [the responsibility for] an unnecessary oath; but one who is too self-confident in handing down legal decisions is a fool, wicked and arrogant of spirit.

[10] *He used to say:* Do not act as judge alone, for none judges alone except One; and do not say, "Accept my view," for they are permitted to, but not you.

[11] *Rabbi Yonasan says:* Whoever fulfills the Torah despite poverty will ultimately fulfill it in wealth; but whoever neglects the Torah because of wealth will ultimately neglect it in poverty.

[12] *Rabbi Meir says:* Reduce your business activities and engage in Torah study. Be of humble spirit before every person. If you should neglect the [study of] Torah, you will come upon many excuses to neglect it; but if you labor in the Torah, God has ample reward to give you.

[13] *Rabbi Eliezer ben Yaakov says:* He who fulfills even a single mitzvah gains himself a single advocate, and he who commits

וְגָזֵל — *Robbery.* As the result of an erroneous legal decision whereby the innocent litigant is deprived of what is legally his.

10. יְחִידִי — *Alone.* Rather, always endeavor to be part of a tribunal, so you will be able to discuss all aspects of the case and render proper judgment.

וְאַל תֹּאמַר — *And do not say.* If you are in the minority, do not insist that your colleagues give in to you, for they, as the majority, can impose their will, and you must accede.

12. בְּטֵלִים הַרְבֵּה — *Many excuses to neglect it.* There are always "compelling reasons" why it is impossible for someone to study Torah. If he weakens his resolve and gives in to "necessity," he will find it harder and harder to study with diligence.

13. קוֹנֶה לוֹ פְּרַקְלִיט אֶחָד — *Gains himself a single advocate,* to plead on his behalf

ד אֶחָד. תְּשׁוּבָה וּמַעֲשִׂים טוֹבִים כִּתְרִיס בִּפְנֵי הַפֻּרְעָנוּת.

[יד] רַבִּי יוֹחָנָן הַסַּנְדְּלָר אוֹמֵר: כָּל כְּנֵסִיָּה שֶׁהִיא לְשֵׁם שָׁמַיִם, סוֹפָהּ לְהִתְקַיֵּם; וְשֶׁאֵינָהּ לְשֵׁם שָׁמַיִם, אֵין סוֹפָהּ לְהִתְקַיֵּם.

[טו] רַבִּי אֶלְעָזָר בֶּן שַׁמּוּעַ אוֹמֵר: יְהִי כְבוֹד תַּלְמִידְךָ חָבִיב עָלֶיךָ כְּשֶׁלָּךְ; וּכְבוֹד חֲבֵרְךָ כְּמוֹרָא רַבָּךְ; וּמוֹרָא רַבָּךְ כְּמוֹרָא שָׁמַיִם.

[טז] רַבִּי יְהוּדָה אוֹמֵר: הֱוֵי זָהִיר בְּתַלְמוּד, שֶׁשִּׁגְגַת תַּלְמוּד עוֹלָה זָדוֹן.

[יז] רַבִּי שִׁמְעוֹן אוֹמֵר: שְׁלֹשָׁה כְתָרִים הֵם: כֶּתֶר תּוֹרָה, וְכֶתֶר כְּהֻנָּה, וְכֶתֶר מַלְכוּת; וְכֶתֶר שֵׁם טוֹב עוֹלֶה עַל גַּבֵּיהֶן.

[יח] רַבִּי נְהוֹרַאי אוֹמֵר: הֱוֵי גוֹלֶה לִמְקוֹם תּוֹרָה, וְאַל תֹּאמַר שֶׁהִיא תָבוֹא אַחֲרֶיךָ, שֶׁחֲבֵרֶיךָ יְקַיְּמוּהָ בְּיָדֶךָ. "וְאֶל בִּינָתְךָ אַל תִּשָּׁעֵן".

[יט] רַבִּי יַנַּאי אוֹמֵר: אֵין בְּיָדֵינוּ לֹא מִשַּׁלְוַת הָרְשָׁעִים וְאַף לֹא מִיִּסּוּרֵי הַצַּדִּיקִים.

[כ] רַבִּי מַתְיָא בֶן חָרָשׁ אוֹמֵר: הֱוֵי מַקְדִּים בִּשְׁלוֹם כָּל אָדָם, וֶהֱוֵי זָנָב לָאֲרָיוֹת, וְאַל תְּהִי רֹאשׁ לַשּׁוּעָלִים.

[כא] רַבִּי יַעֲקֹב אוֹמֵר: הָעוֹלָם הַזֶּה דּוֹמֶה לִפְרוֹזְדוֹר בִּפְנֵי

on the day of judgment.

תְּשׁוּבָה וּמַעֲשִׂים טוֹבִים כִּתְרִיס — *Repentance and good deeds are like a shield.* Life is full of hard times, but if someone constantly seeks to improve himself, God gives him protection from such natural hazards.

14. כָּל כְּנֵסִיָּה שֶׁהִיא לְשֵׁם שָׁמַיִם — *Every assembly that is dedicated to the sake of Heaven.* If the participants sincerely mean to serve God, their undertakings will have eventual success, even though they began on a pessimistic, inauspicious note. Conversely, there is no such guarantee if the motives of the participants are not pure. Consequently, earnest people should not fear failure and criticism — if their intentions are elevated, they will have *ultimate* success.

15. כְּבוֹד תַּלְמִידְךָ — *The honor of your student.* Rendering honor to others is so important that one should always treat them as though they are on a higher level than they really are.

וּמוֹרָא רַבָּךְ — *And the reverence for your teacher.* The comparison of a teacher to God means that one should accept his teacher's opinions even though he disagrees, just as we do not question God's word (*Tiferes Yisrael*).

16. שֶׁשִּׁגְגַת תַּלְמוּד — *For a careless misinterpretation.* A misinterpretation is judged so harshly only if it was due to the student's failure to apply himself according to his capacity. A sincere mistake is regarded as an unintentional error.

17. וְכֶתֶר שֵׁם טוֹב — *But the crown of a*

4 *even a single transgression gains himself a single accuser. Repentance and good deeds are like a shield against retribution.*

[14] *Rabbi Yochanan the Sandler says: Every assembly that is dedicated to the sake of Heaven will have an enduring effect, but one that is not for the sake of Heaven will not have an enduring effect.*

[15] *Rabbi Elazar ben Shamua says: Let the honor of your student be as dear to you as your own; the honor of your colleague as the reverence for your teacher; and the reverence for your teacher as the reverence of Heaven.*

[16] *Rabbi Yehudah says: Be meticulous in study, for a careless misinterpretation is considered tantamount to willful transgression.*

[17] *Rabbi Shimon says: There are three crowns — the crown of Torah, the crown of priesthood, and the crown of kingship; but the crown of a good name surpasses them all.*

[18] *Rabbi Nehorai says: Exile yourself to a place of Torah — and do not assume that it will come after you — for it is your colleagues who will cause it to remain with you; "and do not rely on your own understanding" (Proverbs 3:5).*

[19] *Rabbi Yannai says: It is not in our power to explain either the tranquility of the wicked or the suffering of the righteous.*

[20] *Rabbi Masya ben Charash says: Initiate a greeting to every person; and be a tail to lions rather than a head to foxes.*

[21] *Rabbi Yaakov says: This World is like a corridor before the World*

good name. This crown adorns someone whose deeds and behavior earn him the respect and affection of his fellows. Even scholars, priests, and kings are lacking if they fail to earn this crown.

18. הֱוֵי גוֹלֶה לִמְקוֹם תּוֹרָה — *Exile yourself to a place of Torah.* One should uproot himself and move to a place where there are Torah scholars from whom to learn and be stimulated.

שֶׁהִיא תָבוֹא אַחֲרֶיךָ — *That it will come after you.* That the Torah (i.e., scholars) will follow you if you move to a place currently devoid of Torah.

שֶׁחֲבֵרֶיךָ יְקַיְּמוּהָ בְּיָדֶךָ — *For it is your colleagues* [through stimulating debate] *who will cause it to remain with you.* According to *Rashi*, this explains the beginning of the mishnah: One must live in a Torah environment because it is only in association with fellow students

that Torah can be properly studied.

אַל תִּשָּׁעֵן — *Do not rely,* by studying alone, in an environment devoid of Torah scholarship.

19. אֵין בְּיָדֵינוּ — *It is not in our power.* We cannot know for sure if what befalls each of them is indeed a blessing or a calamity. We must therefore abstain from passing judgment in either case and not permit our own short-sighted view of events to influence our decisions (*R' Hirsch*).

20. וֶהֱוֵי זָנָב לָאֲרָיוֹת — *And be a tail to lions.* Better to be a follower of the righteous (from whom you can learn) than a leader of common people.

21. In the Talmud (*Avodah Zarah* 3a) there is a similar saying: "This World is like the eve of Sabbath, and the World to Come is like Sabbath. He who prepares on the eve of Sabbath will have

ד הָעוֹלָם הַבָּא, הַתְקֵן עַצְמְךָ בַּפְּרוֹזְדוֹר, כְּדֵי שֶׁתִּכָּנֵס לַטְּרַקְלִין.

[כב] הוּא הָיָה אוֹמֵר: יָפָה שָׁעָה אַחַת בִּתְשׁוּבָה וּמַעֲשִׂים טוֹבִים בָּעוֹלָם הַזֶּה מִכָּל חַיֵּי הָעוֹלָם הַבָּא; וְיָפָה שָׁעָה אַחַת שֶׁל קוֹרַת רוּחַ בָּעוֹלָם הַבָּא מִכָּל חַיֵּי הָעוֹלָם הַזֶּה.

[כג] רַבִּי שִׁמְעוֹן בֶּן אֶלְעָזָר אוֹמֵר: אַל תְּרַצֶּה אֶת חֲבֵרְךָ בִּשְׁעַת כַּעֲסוֹ; וְאַל תְּנַחֲמֶהוּ בְּשָׁעָה שֶׁמֵּתוֹ מֻטָּל לְפָנָיו; וְאַל תִּשְׁאַל לוֹ בִּשְׁעַת נִדְרוֹ; וְאַל תִּשְׁתַּדֵּל לִרְאוֹתוֹ בִּשְׁעַת קַלְקָלָתוֹ.

[כד] שְׁמוּאֵל הַקָּטָן אוֹמֵר: ,,בִּנְפֹל אוֹיִבְךָ אַל תִּשְׂמָח, וּבִכָּשְׁלוֹ אַל יָגֵל לִבֶּךָ. פֶּן יִרְאֶה יהוה וְרַע בְּעֵינָיו, וְהֵשִׁיב מֵעָלָיו אַפּוֹ''.

[כה] אֱלִישָׁע בֶּן אֲבוּיָה אוֹמֵר: הַלּוֹמֵד יֶלֶד, לְמָה הוּא דוֹמֶה? לִדְיוֹ כְתוּבָה עַל נְיָר חָדָשׁ. וְהַלּוֹמֵד זָקֵן, לְמָה הוּא דוֹמֶה? לִדְיוֹ כְתוּבָה עַל נְיָר מָחוּק.

[כו] רַבִּי יוֹסֵי בַּר יְהוּדָה אִישׁ כְּפַר הַבַּבְלִי אוֹמֵר: הַלּוֹמֵד מִן הַקְּטַנִּים, לְמָה הוּא דוֹמֶה? לְאוֹכֵל עֲנָבִים קֵהוֹת, וְשׁוֹתֶה יַיִן מִגִּתּוֹ. וְהַלּוֹמֵד מִן הַזְּקֵנִים, לְמָה הוּא דוֹמֶה? לְאוֹכֵל עֲנָבִים בְּשׁוּלוֹת, וְשׁוֹתֶה יַיִן יָשָׁן.

[כז] רַבִּי מֵאִיר אוֹמֵר: אַל תִּסְתַּכֵּל בַּקַּנְקַן, אֶלָּא בַּמֶּה שֶׁיֵּשׁ בּוֹ; יֵשׁ קַנְקַן חָדָשׁ מָלֵא יָשָׁן, וְיָשָׁן שֶׁאֲפִילוּ חָדָשׁ אֵין בּוֹ.

[כח] רַבִּי אֶלְעָזָר הַקַּפָּר אוֹמֵר: הַקִּנְאָה וְהַתַּאֲוָה וְהַכָּבוֹד מוֹצִיאִין אֶת הָאָדָם מִן הָעוֹלָם.

[כט] הוּא הָיָה אוֹמֵר: הַיִּלּוֹדִים לָמוּת, וְהַמֵּתִים לִחְיוֹת, וְהַחַיִּים לִדּוֹן — לֵידַע לְהוֹדִיעַ וּלְהִוָּדַע שֶׁהוּא אֵל, הוּא הַיּוֹצֵר, הוּא הַבּוֹרֵא, הוּא הַמֵּבִין, הוּא הַדַּיָּן, הוּא הָעֵד, הוּא בַּעַל דִּין,

food to eat on Sabbath."

22. יָפָה שָׁעָה אַחַת — *Better one hour.* The mishnah deals with two different concepts. Only in This World can one elevate himself spiritually; in the World to Come he can only enjoy the reward for his accomplishments here. On the other hand, all the bliss of all the generations in the history of the world cannot equal an hour of bliss in the World to Come.

23. אַל תְּרַצֶּה — *Do not appease.* R' Shimon ben Elazar's message concerns the importance of proper timing. To reason with or appease someone at a time of great passion is counterproductive.

24. בִּנְפֹל אוֹיִבְךָ — *When your enemy falls.* This entire dictum is a quotation from

4 to Come; prepare yourself in the corridor so that you may enter the banquet hall.

[22] He used to say: Better one hour of repentance and good deeds in This World than the entire life of the World to Come; and better one hour of spiritual bliss in the World to Come than the entire life of This World.

[23] *Rabbi Shimon ben Elazar says:* Do not appease your fellow in the time of his anger; do not console him while his dead lies before him; do not question him about his vow at the time he makes it; and do not attempt to see him at the time of his degradation.

[24] *Shmuel HaKattan says:* "When your enemy falls be not glad, and when he stumbles let your heart not be joyous. Lest HASHEM see and it displease Him, and He will turn His wrath from him [to you]' (Proverbs 24:17-18).

[25] *Elisha ben Avuyah says:* One who studies Torah as a child, to what can he be likened? — to ink written on fresh paper. And one who studies Torah as an old man, to what can he be likened? — to ink written on smudged paper.

[26] *Rabbi Yose bar Yehudah of Kfar HaBavli says:* One who learns Torah from the young, to what can he be likened? — to one who eats unripe grapes or drinks unfermented wine from his vat. But one who learns Torah from the old, to what can he be likened? — to one who eats ripe grapes or drinks aged wine.

[27] *Rabbi Meir says:* Do not look at the vessel, but what is in it; there is a new vessel filled with old wine and an old vessel that does not even contain new wine.

[28] *Rabbi Elazar HaKappar says:* Jealousy, lust, and glory remove a man from the world.

[29] He used to say: The newborn will die; the dead will live again; the living will be judged — in order that they know, teach, and become aware that He is God, He is the Fashioner, He is the Creator, He is the Discerner, He is the Judge, He is the Witness, He is the

---

the Book of *Proverbs*. Shmuel HaKattan apparently was in the habit of quoting it when admonishing people.

25. גְּוִיל חָדָשׁ — *Fresh paper*, which retains ink legibly and permanently. This is a lesson on a person's duty to learn Torah while he is young and his mind is fresh and receptive.

27. אַל תִּסְתַּכֵּל בַּקַּנְקַן — *Do not look at the vessel*. This contrasts with the view

in mishnah 26. Do not draw general conclusions based on age; some young men have achieved greater levels of learning than older men. Also, one should not judge others only by their appearance.

28. הַקִּנְאָה וְהַתַּאֲוָה וְהַכָּבוֹד — *Jealousy, lust, and glory.* These base instincts and appetites prevent a person from enjoying life.

ד הוּא עָתִיד לָדוּן. בָּרוּךְ הוּא, שֶׁאֵין לְפָנָיו לֹא עַוְלָה, וְלֹא שִׁכְחָה, וְלֹא מַשּׂוֹא פָנִים, וְלֹא מִקַּח שֹׁחַד; שֶׁהַכֹּל שֶׁלּוֹ. וְדַע, שֶׁהַכֹּל לְפִי הַחֶשְׁבּוֹן. וְאַל יַבְטִיחֲךָ יִצְרְךָ שֶׁהַשְּׁאוֹל בֵּית מָנוֹס לָךְ — שֶׁעַל כָּרְחֲךָ אַתָּה נוֹצָר; וְעַל כָּרְחֲךָ אַתָּה נוֹלָד; וְעַל כָּרְחֲךָ אַתָּה חַי; וְעַל כָּרְחֲךָ אַתָּה מֵת; וְעַל כָּרְחֲךָ אַתָּה עָתִיד לִתֵּן דִּין וְחֶשְׁבּוֹן לִפְנֵי מֶלֶךְ מַלְכֵי הַמְּלָכִים, הַקָּדוֹשׁ בָּרוּךְ הוּא.

※ ※ ※

רַבִּי חֲנַנְיָא בֶּן עֲקַשְׁיָא אוֹמֵר: רָצָה הַקָּדוֹשׁ בָּרוּךְ הוּא לְזַכּוֹת אֶת יִשְׂרָאֵל, לְפִיכָךְ הִרְבָּה לָהֶם תּוֹרָה וּמִצְוֹת, שֶׁנֶּאֱמַר: ״יהוה חָפֵץ לְמַעַן צִדְקוֹ, יַגְדִּיל תּוֹרָה וְיַאְדִּיר״.

◆§ פרק חמישי ◆§

ה כָּל יִשְׂרָאֵל יֵשׁ לָהֶם חֵלֶק לָעוֹלָם הַבָּא, שֶׁנֶּאֱמַר: ״וְעַמֵּךְ כֻּלָּם צַדִּיקִים, לְעוֹלָם יִירְשׁוּ אָרֶץ, נֵצֶר מַטָּעַי, מַעֲשֵׂה יָדַי לְהִתְפָּאֵר״.

※ ※ ※

[א] **בַּעֲשָׂרָה** מַאֲמָרוֹת נִבְרָא הָעוֹלָם. וּמַה תַּלְמוּד לוֹמַר? וַהֲלֹא בְמַאֲמָר אֶחָד יָכוֹל לְהִבָּרְאוֹת? אֶלָּא לְהִפָּרַע מִן הָרְשָׁעִים, שֶׁמְּאַבְּדִין אֶת הָעוֹלָם שֶׁנִּבְרָא בַּעֲשָׂרָה מַאֲמָרוֹת, וְלִתֵּן שָׂכָר טוֹב לַצַּדִּיקִים, שֶׁמְּקַיְּמִין אֶת הָעוֹלָם שֶׁנִּבְרָא בַּעֲשָׂרָה מַאֲמָרוֹת.

[ב] עֲשָׂרָה דוֹרוֹת מֵאָדָם וְעַד נֹחַ, לְהוֹדִיעַ כַּמָּה אֶרֶךְ אַפַּיִם לְפָנָיו; שֶׁכָּל הַדּוֹרוֹת הָיוּ מַכְעִיסִין וּבָאִין, עַד שֶׁהֵבִיא עֲלֵיהֶם אֶת מֵי הַמַּבּוּל.

[ג] עֲשָׂרָה דוֹרוֹת מִנֹּחַ וְעַד אַבְרָהָם, לְהוֹדִיעַ כַּמָּה אֶרֶךְ אַפַּיִם לְפָנָיו; שֶׁכָּל הַדּוֹרוֹת הָיוּ מַכְעִיסִין וּבָאִין, עַד שֶׁבָּא אַבְרָהָם אָבִינוּ וְקִבֵּל שְׂכַר כֻּלָּם.

[ד] עֲשָׂרָה נִסְיוֹנוֹת נִתְנַסָּה אַבְרָהָם אָבִינוּ וְעָמַד בְּכֻלָּם, לְהוֹדִיעַ כַּמָּה חִבָּתוֹ שֶׁל אַבְרָהָם אָבִינוּ.

CHAPTER FIVE

1-3. The ten utterances are recorded in *Genesis* 1 and in 2:18.

The generations from Adam to Noah are enumerated in *Genesis* 5.

The generations from Noah to Abraham are listed in *Genesis* 5.

4 *Plaintiff, He will judge. Blessed is He, before Whom there is no iniquity, no forgetfulness, no favoritism, and no acceptance of bribery, for everything is His. Know that everything is according to the reckoning. And let not your Evil Inclination promise you that the grave will be an escape for you — for against your will you were created; against your will you were born; against your will you live; against your will you die, and against your will you are destined to give an account before the King Who rules over kings, the Holy One, Blessed is He.*

❦ ❦ ❦

Rabbi Chanania ben Akashia says: The Holy One, Blessed is He, wished to confer merit upon Israel; therefore He gave them Torah and mitzvos in abundance, as it is said: "HASHEM desired, for the sake of its [Israel's] righteousness, that the Torah be made great and glorious" (Isaiah 42:21).

5 ⊰§{ CHAPTER FIVE }§⊱

All Israel has a share in the World to Come, as it is said: "And your people are all righteous; they shall inherit the land forever; they are the branch of My planting, My handiwork, in which to take pride" (Isaiah 60:21).

❦ ❦ ❦

[1] **בַּעֲשָׂרָה** *With ten utterances the world was created. What does this come to teach us? Indeed, could it not have been created with one utterance? This was to exact punishment from the wicked who destroy the world that was created with ten utterances, and to bestow goodly reward upon the righteous who sustain the world that was created by ten utterances.*

[2] *There were ten generations from Adam to Noah — to show the degree of His patience; for all those generations angered Him increasingly, until He brought upon them the waters of the Flood.*

[3] *There were ten generations from Noah to Abraham — to show the degree of His patience; for all those generations angered Him increasingly, until our forefather Abraham came and received the reward of them all.*

[4] *Our forefather Abraham was tested with ten trials, and he withstood them all — to show the degree of our forefather Abraham's love for God.*

The generations from Noah to Abraham are listed in *Genesis* 11. The count there begins with Noah's son Shem.

וְקִבֵּל שָׂכָר כֻּלָּם — *And received the reward of them all.* Abraham was so righteous that he received the total reward that would have gone to the ten generations, had they not been sinful.

4. עֲשָׂרָה נִסְיוֹנוֹת — *Ten trials.* See footnote to ArtScroll *Bereishis* 12:1, page 424.

[ה] עֲשָׂרָה נִסִּים נַעֲשׂוּ לַאֲבוֹתֵינוּ בְּמִצְרַיִם, וַעֲשָׂרָה עַל הַיָּם. עֶשֶׂר מַכּוֹת הֵבִיא הַקָּדוֹשׁ בָּרוּךְ הוּא עַל הַמִּצְרִים בְּמִצְרַיִם, וְעֶשֶׂר עַל הַיָּם.

[ו] עֲשָׂרָה נִסְיוֹנוֹת נִסּוּ אֲבוֹתֵינוּ אֶת הַקָּדוֹשׁ בָּרוּךְ הוּא בַּמִּדְבָּר, שֶׁנֶּאֱמַר: ״וַיְנַסּוּ אֹתִי זֶה עֶשֶׂר פְּעָמִים, וְלֹא שָׁמְעוּ בְּקוֹלִי״.

[ז] עֲשָׂרָה נִסִּים נַעֲשׂוּ לַאֲבוֹתֵינוּ בְּבֵית הַמִּקְדָּשׁ: לֹא הִפִּילָה אִשָּׁה מֵרֵיחַ בְּשַׂר הַקֹּדֶשׁ; וְלֹא הִסְרִיחַ בְּשַׂר הַקֹּדֶשׁ מֵעוֹלָם; וְלֹא נִרְאָה זְבוּב בְּבֵית הַמִּטְבָּחַיִם; וְלֹא אֵרַע קֶרִי לְכֹהֵן גָּדוֹל בְּיוֹם הַכִּפּוּרִים; וְלֹא כִבּוּ הַגְּשָׁמִים אֵשׁ שֶׁל עֲצֵי הַמַּעֲרָכָה; וְלֹא נִצְּחָה הָרוּחַ אֶת עַמּוּד הֶעָשָׁן; וְלֹא נִמְצָא פְסוּל בָּעֹמֶר, וּבִשְׁתֵּי הַלֶּחֶם, וּבְלֶחֶם הַפָּנִים; עוֹמְדִים צְפוּפִים, וּמִשְׁתַּחֲוִים רְוָחִים; וְלֹא הִזִּיק נָחָשׁ וְעַקְרָב בִּירוּשָׁלַיִם מֵעוֹלָם; וְלֹא אָמַר אָדָם לַחֲבֵרוֹ: ״צַר לִי הַמָּקוֹם שֶׁאָלִין בִּירוּשָׁלַיִם״.

[ח] עֲשָׂרָה דְבָרִים נִבְרְאוּ בְּעֶרֶב שַׁבָּת בֵּין הַשְּׁמָשׁוֹת, וְאֵלּוּ הֵן: פִּי הָאָרֶץ, וּפִי הַבְּאֵר, פִּי הָאָתוֹן, וְהַקֶּשֶׁת, וְהַמָּן, וְהַמַּטֶּה, וְהַשָּׁמִיר, הַכְּתָב, וְהַמִּכְתָּב, וְהַלּוּחוֹת. וְיֵשׁ אוֹמְרִים:

---

5. עֲשָׂרָה נִסִּים ... לַאֲבוֹתֵינוּ בְּמִצְרַיִם — *Ten miracles ... for our ancestors in Egypt*, i.e., by being saved from the ten plagues which were brought upon the Egyptians. Thus, each plague was accompanied by the miracle of Jewish salvation.

7. בְּבֵית הַמִּקְדָּשׁ — *In the Holy Temple*, the abode of the Divine Presence, where the laws of nature were transcended.

בְּשַׂר הַקֹּדֶשׁ — *Sacrificial meat*. Flesh of the offerings were burned constantly on the Altar and for the meals of the *Kohanim*. The miracle was that no pregnant woman ever craved to eat this meat, for it would not be permitted to her and she might otherwise miscarry if her craving were not satisfied.

קֶרִי — *Seminal emission*, which would have rendered the priest ritually contaminated and unfit to officiate in the Temple.

בָּעֹמֶר — *In the Omer* (see *Leviticus* 23:19). The sheaf of barley offered in the Temple on the morning of the 16th of Nissan, after which people were allowed to eat the new grain crop. A limited amount of barley was cut on the night before (the second night of Passover) and offered the following morning. Had a ritual defect been found in the barley, the offering could not be brought that year.

וּבִשְׁתֵּי הַלֶּחֶם — *Or in the Two Loaves*. (See *Leviticus* 23:17.) These had to be baked before the onset of Shavuos, and offered on the festival itself. If they became disqualified by a defect, replacements could not be baked.

וּבְלֶחֶם הַפָּנִים — *Or in the Showbread*. (See *Exodus* 25:30; *Leviticus* 24:5.) Twelve loaves were baked each Friday and placed on the Table in the Temple on the Sabbath, where they remained until new loaves replaced them on the following Sabbath. If a defect were found, the *mitzvah* could not be performed because new loaves could not be baked on the Sabbath.

5 [5] *Ten miracles were performed for our ancestors in Egypt and ten at the Sea. Ten plagues did the Holy One, Blessed is He, bring upon the Egyptians in Egypt and ten at the Sea.*

[6] *With ten trials did our ancestors test the Holy One, Blessed is He, in the Wilderness, as it is said: "They have tested Me these ten times and did not heed My voice" (Numbers 14:22).*

[7] *Ten miracles were performed for our ancestors in the Holy Temple: No woman miscarried because of the aroma of the sacrificial meat; the sacrificial meat never became putrid; no fly was seen in the place where the meat was butchered; no seminal emission occurred to the High Priest on Yom Kippur; the rains did not extinguish the fire on the Altar-pyre; the wind did not disperse the vertical column of smoke from the Altar; no disqualification was found in the Omer, or in the Two Loaves, or in the Showbread; the people stood crowded together, yet prostrated themselves in ample space; neither serpent nor scorpion ever caused injury in Jerusalem; nor did any man say to his fellow, "The space is insufficient for me to stay overnight in Jerusalem."*

[8] *Ten things were created on Sabbath eve, at twilight. They are: The mouth of the earth; the mouth of the well; the mouth of the donkey; the rainbow [which was Noah's sign that there would be no future floods]; the manna; the staff; the shamir worm; the script; the inscrip-*

צְפוּפִים — *Crowded together.* Throngs of pilgrims gathered in the Temple Courtyard on the Festivals and Yom Kippur, filling it to capacity. Yet miraculously, though there was not even enough room to stand, each person had ample room to prostrate himself and confess his sins on Yom Kippur or to recite private prayers on the Festivals without being overheard by his neighbor.

צַר לִי הַמָּקוֹם — *The space is insufficient for me;* i.e., there is no room for me. Though throngs of people came to Jerusalem, especially for the Festivals, there were sufficient accommodations for them all. Moreover, because of the holiness of the city, God provided for all residents of Jerusalem so that no one ever had to move to another city to seek a livelihood.

8. Even the provision for future miracles and exceptions to God's natural order were provided for in advance when He created the world, immediately prior to the first Sabbath.

פִּי הָאָרֶץ — *The mouth of the earth,* which engulfed Korah and his fellow conspirators (*Numbers* 16:32).

וּפִי הַבְּאֵר — *The mouth of the well,* which provided water for Israel in the Wilderness.

פִּי הָאָתוֹן — *The mouth of the donkey,* which spoke to Balaam (*Numbers* 22:28).

הַמַּטֶּה — *The staff,* with which Moses performed the signs in Egypt (*Exodus* 4:17). According to Rabbinic tradition it belonged to Adam and was transmitted through the generations to Moses. The Four-letter Divine Name was engraved on it.

וְהַשָּׁמִיר — *The shamir worm,* a small worm that, according to the Mishnah, split large stones as it crawled on them. Since no sword or iron — symbols of violence — could be used to hew the stones for the Temple's construction, the *shamir* took the place of conventional tools.

הַכְּתָב — *The script,* the form of the Hebrew alphabet (*Rashi*).

וְהַמִּכְתָּב — *The inscription,* the instru-

ה אַף הַמַּזִּיקִין, וּקְבוּרָתוֹ שֶׁל מֹשֶׁה, וְאֵילוֹ שֶׁל אַבְרָהָם אָבִינוּ. וְיֵשׁ אוֹמְרִים: אַף צְבָת בִּצְבָת עֲשׂוּיָה.

[ט] שִׁבְעָה דְבָרִים בַּגֹּלֶם, וְשִׁבְעָה בֶּחָכָם. חָכָם אֵינוֹ מְדַבֵּר לִפְנֵי מִי שֶׁגָּדוֹל מִמֶּנּוּ בְּחָכְמָה וּבְמִנְיָן; וְאֵינוֹ נִכְנָס לְתוֹךְ דִּבְרֵי חֲבֵרוֹ; וְאֵינוֹ נִבְהָל לְהָשִׁיב; שׁוֹאֵל כְּעִנְיָן, וּמֵשִׁיב כַּהֲלָכָה; וְאוֹמֵר עַל רִאשׁוֹן רִאשׁוֹן, וְעַל אַחֲרוֹן אַחֲרוֹן, וְעַל מַה שֶּׁלֹּא שָׁמַע אוֹמֵר: "לֹא שָׁמַעְתִּי"; וּמוֹדֶה עַל הָאֱמֶת. וְחִלּוּפֵיהֶן בַּגֹּלֶם.

[י] שִׁבְעָה מִינֵי פֻרְעָנִיּוֹת בָּאִין לָעוֹלָם עַל שִׁבְעָה גוּפֵי עֲבֵרָה: מִקְצָתָן מְעַשְּׂרִין וּמִקְצָתָן אֵינָן מְעַשְּׂרִין — רָעָב שֶׁל בַּצֹּרֶת בָּא, מִקְצָתָן רְעֵבִים וּמִקְצָתָן שְׂבֵעִים; גָּמְרוּ שֶׁלֹּא לְעַשֵּׂר — רָעָב שֶׁל מְהוּמָה וְשֶׁל בַּצֹּרֶת בָּא; וְשֶׁלֹּא לִטֹּל אֶת הַחַלָּה — רָעָב שֶׁל כְּלָיָה בָּא;

[יא] דֶּבֶר בָּא לָעוֹלָם — עַל מִיתוֹת הָאֲמוּרוֹת בַּתּוֹרָה שֶׁלֹּא נִמְסְרוּ לְבֵית דִּין, וְעַל פֵּרוֹת שְׁבִיעִית; חֶרֶב בָּאָה לָעוֹלָם — עַל עִנּוּי הַדִּין, וְעַל עִוּוּת הַדִּין, וְעַל הַמּוֹרִים בַּתּוֹרָה שֶׁלֹּא כַהֲלָכָה; חַיָּה רָעָה בָּאָה לָעוֹלָם — עַל שְׁבוּעַת שָׁוְא, וְעַל חִלּוּל הַשֵּׁם; גָּלוּת בָּאָה לָעוֹלָם — עַל עוֹבְדֵי עֲבוֹדָה זָרָה, וְעַל גִּלּוּי עֲרָיוֹת, וְעַל שְׁפִיכוּת דָּמִים, וְעַל שְׁמִטַּת הָאָרֶץ.

[יב] בְּאַרְבָּעָה פְרָקִים הַדֶּבֶר מִתְרַבֶּה: בָּרְבִיעִית, וּבַשְּׁבִיעִית, וּבְמוֹצָאֵי שְׁבִיעִית, וּבְמוֹצָאֵי הֶחָג שֶׁבְּכָל שָׁנָה וְשָׁנָה. בָּרְבִיעִית, מִפְּנֵי מַעְשַׂר עָנִי שֶׁבַּשְּׁלִישִׁית; בַּשְּׁבִיעִית, מִפְּנֵי מַעְשַׂר עָנִי שֶׁבַּשִּׁשִּׁית; בְּמוֹצָאֵי שְׁבִיעִית, מִפְּנֵי פֵרוֹת שְׁבִיעִית; בְּמוֹצָאֵי הֶחָג שֶׁבְּכָל שָׁנָה וְשָׁנָה, מִפְּנֵי גֶזֶל מַתְּנוֹת עֲנִיִּים.

ment used by God to engrave the לוחות, *Tablets*, of the Ten Commandments, which were miraculously "written on both their sides" (*Exodus* 32:15).

וְהַלּוּחוֹת — *And the Tablets.* The first Tablets were created on the first Sabbath eve, but the second ones were carved by Moses.

אַף צְבָת בִּצְבָת עֲשׂוּיָה — *Also tongs, which are made with tongs.* Tongs are made with another pair which holds the red-hot metal for the smith. According to this view, God provided man with the original pair of tongs with which to make others.

9. רִאשׁוֹן רִאשׁוֹן — *First things first.* His mind works in an orderly, organized fashion.

"לֹא שָׁמַעְתִּי" — *"I have not heard."* He does not fabricate false sources, nor is he ashamed to admit his ignorance.

וּמוֹדֶה עַל הָאֱמֶת — *And he acknowledges the truth.* He readily admits an error.

10-11. Seven forms of Divine retribu-

[46] פרקי אבות / פרק ה

5 tion; and the Tablets. Some say also destructive spirits, Moses' grave, and the ram of our forefather Abraham. And some say also tongs, which are made with tongs.

[9] *Seven traits characterize an uncultivated person and seven a learned one. A learned person does not begin speaking before one who is greater than he in wisdom or in years; he does not interrupt the words of his fellow; he does not answer impetuously; he questions with relevance to the subject and he replies accurately; he discusses first things first and last things last; about something he has not heard he says, "I have not heard"; and he acknowledges the truth. And the reverse of these characterize an uncultivated person.*

[10] *Seven kinds of punishment come to the world for seven kinds of transgressions. (a) If some people tithe and others do not, a famine caused by lack of rain ensues, some go hungry and others are satisfied; (b) if all decided not to tithe, general famine caused by both armed bands and drought ensues; and (c) [if they also decided] not to separate the challah, a famine caused by destructive drought ensues;*

[11] *(d) pestilence comes to the world for the death penalties prescribed by the Torah that were not carried out by the court, and for illegally using the fruits of the Sabbatical year; (e) the sword of war comes to the world for the delay of justice, for the perversion of justice, and for interpreting the Torah decision in opposition to the halachah; (f) wild beasts come upon the world for vain oaths and for desecration of God's Name; (g) exile comes to the world for idolatry, for immorality, for bloodshed, and for working the earth during the Sabbatical year.*

[12] *At four periods [of the seven-year Sabbatical cycle] pestilence increases — in the fourth year, in the seventh year, in the year following the Sabbatical year, and annually following the Succos Festival. In the fourth year, for [neglecting] the tithe of the poor in the third; in the seventh year, for [neglecting] the tithe of the poor in the sixth; in the year following the Sabbatical year, for [violating the laws of] the Sabbatical produce; annually, at the conclusion of the Festival of Succos, for robbing the poor of their gifts.*

tion — "measure for measure" — for seven sins. Every calamity that befalls mankind is a punishment for sin.

12. This mishnah elaborates on one of the themes of the preceding one, the sending of a Plague (דֶּבֶר, *pestilence*) upon the earth. As noted previously, pestilence strikes the world for a variety of sins. Even at such times, however, the people dare not neglect their responsibilities to the poor. If they do, the pestilence would intensify. The special times of responsibility to the poor are at the harvests of the third and sixth years, when a tithe is to be given to the poor, and during the Sabbatical year, when everyone, including the poor, is entitled to take whatever grew in the fields during the year.

גֶּזֶל מַתְּנוֹת עֲנִיִּים — *For robbing the poor of their gifts.* At harvest time, which is before Succos, the Torah requires farmers to leave dropped and forgotten sheaves and a corner of the field for the poor.

ה [יג] אַרְבַּע מִדּוֹת בָּאָדָם: הָאוֹמֵר: "שֶׁלִּי שֶׁלִּי וְשֶׁלְּךָ שֶׁלָּךְ", זוֹ מִדָּה בֵינוֹנִית, וְיֵשׁ אוֹמְרִים: זוֹ מִדַּת סְדוֹם; "שֶׁלִּי שֶׁלְּךָ וְשֶׁלְּךָ שֶׁלִּי", עַם הָאָרֶץ; "שֶׁלִּי שֶׁלְּךָ וְשֶׁלְּךָ שֶׁלָּךְ", חָסִיד; "שֶׁלְּךָ שֶׁלִּי וְשֶׁלִּי שֶׁלִּי", רָשָׁע.

[יד] אַרְבַּע מִדּוֹת בְּדֵעוֹת: נוֹחַ לִכְעוֹס וְנוֹחַ לִרְצוֹת, יָצָא שְׂכָרוֹ בְּהֶפְסֵדוֹ; קָשֶׁה לִכְעוֹס וְקָשֶׁה לִרְצוֹת, יָצָא הֶפְסֵדוֹ בִּשְׂכָרוֹ; קָשֶׁה לִכְעוֹס וְנוֹחַ לִרְצוֹת, חָסִיד; נוֹחַ לִכְעוֹס וְקָשֶׁה לִרְצוֹת, רָשָׁע.

[טו] אַרְבַּע מִדּוֹת בְּתַלְמִידִים: מָהִיר לִשְׁמוֹעַ וּמָהִיר לְאַבֵּד, יָצָא שְׂכָרוֹ בְּהֶפְסֵדוֹ; קָשֶׁה לִשְׁמוֹעַ וְקָשֶׁה לְאַבֵּד, יָצָא הֶפְסֵדוֹ בִּשְׂכָרוֹ; מָהִיר לִשְׁמוֹעַ וְקָשֶׁה לְאַבֵּד, זֶה חֵלֶק טוֹב; קָשֶׁה לִשְׁמוֹעַ וּמָהִיר לְאַבֵּד, זֶה חֵלֶק רַע.

[טז] אַרְבַּע מִדּוֹת בְּנוֹתְנֵי צְדָקָה: הָרוֹצֶה שֶׁיִּתֵּן וְלֹא יִתְּנוּ אֲחֵרִים, עֵינוֹ רָעָה בְּשֶׁל אֲחֵרִים; יִתְּנוּ אֲחֵרִים וְהוּא לֹא יִתֵּן, עֵינוֹ רָעָה בְּשֶׁלּוֹ; יִתֵּן וְיִתְּנוּ אֲחֵרִים, חָסִיד; לֹא יִתֵּן וְלֹא יִתְּנוּ אֲחֵרִים, רָשָׁע.

[יז] אַרְבַּע מִדּוֹת בְּהוֹלְכֵי בֵית הַמִּדְרָשׁ: הוֹלֵךְ וְאֵינוֹ עוֹשֶׂה, שְׂכַר הֲלִיכָה בְּיָדוֹ; עוֹשֶׂה וְאֵינוֹ הוֹלֵךְ, שְׂכַר מַעֲשֶׂה בְּיָדוֹ; הוֹלֵךְ וְעוֹשֶׂה, חָסִיד; לֹא הוֹלֵךְ וְלֹא עוֹשֶׂה, רָשָׁע.

[יח] אַרְבַּע מִדּוֹת בְּיוֹשְׁבִים לִפְנֵי חֲכָמִים: סְפוֹג, וּמַשְׁפֵּךְ, מְשַׁמֶּרֶת, וְנָפָה. סְפוֹג, שֶׁהוּא סוֹפֵג אֶת הַכֹּל; וּמַשְׁפֵּךְ, שֶׁמַּכְנִיס בְּזוֹ וּמוֹצִיא בְזוֹ; מְשַׁמֶּרֶת, שֶׁמּוֹצִיאָה אֶת הַיַּיִן וְקוֹלֶטֶת אֶת הַשְּׁמָרִים; וְנָפָה, שֶׁמּוֹצִיאָה אֶת הַקֶּמַח וְקוֹלֶטֶת אֶת הַסֹּלֶת.

13. זוֹ מִדַּת סְדוֹם — *This is characteristic of Sodom,* whose residents displayed the epitome of selfishness — *"She did not strengthen the hand of the needy"* (Ezekiel 16:49). According to this view, having an attitude of "each man for himself" is not merely average, but unethical, since it negates the entire concept of charity and benevolence.

14. נוֹחַ לִכְעוֹס ... יָצָא שְׂכָרוֹ בְּהֶפְסֵדוֹ — *One who is angered easily ... his gain is offset by his loss.* (This is the version cited by Rashi.) The positive aspect of such a person's character is offset by the negative aspect of his being easily provoked; a moment of anger causes damage that cannot be erased by easy subsequent appeasement.

16. עֵינוֹ רָעָה בְּשֶׁל אֲחֵרִים — *He begrudges* [lit., *his eye is evil with regard to*] *others.* He does not want them to accrue merit and blessing for their charitable act; alternatively: He begrudges the needy any extra charity.

5 [13] *There are four character types among people: (a) One who says, "My property is mine and yours is yours," is an average character type, but some say this is characteristic of Sodom; (b) "Mine is yours, and yours is mine," is an unlearned person; (c) "Mine is yours and yours is yours," is scrupulously pious; (d) "Yours is mine and mine is mine," is wicked.*

[14] *There are four types of temperament: (a) One who is angered easily and pacified easily, his gain is offset by his loss; (b) one who is hard to anger and hard to pacify, his loss is offset by his gain; (c) one who is hard to anger and easy to pacify is pious; (d) one who is easily angered and hard to pacify is wicked.*

[15] *There are four types of students: (a) One who grasps quickly and forgets quickly, his gain is offset by his loss; (b) one who grasps slowly and forgets slowly, his loss is offset by his gain; (c) one who grasps quickly and forgets slowly, this is a good portion; (d) one who grasps slowly and forgets quickly, this is a bad portion.*

[16] *There are four types of donors to charity: (a) One who wishes to give himself but wants others not to give, he begrudges others; (b) that others should give but that he should not give, he begrudges himself; (c) that he should give and that others should give is pious; (d) that he should not give and that others should not give is wicked.*

[17] *There are four types among those who go to the house of study: (a) One who goes but does not study has the reward for going; (b) one who studies [at home] but does not attend [the house of study] has the reward for accomplishment; (c) one who goes and studies is pious; (d) one who does not go and does not study is wicked.*

[18] *There are four types among students who sit before the sages: A sponge, a funnel, a strainer, and a sieve: a sponge, which absorbs everything; a funnel, which lets in from one end and lets out from the other; a strainer, which lets the wine flow through and retains the sediment; and a sieve, which allows the flour dust to pass through and retains the fine flour.*

עֵינוֹ רָעָה בְּשֶׁלּוֹ — *He begrudges himself.* He begrudges himself the merit that would accrue to him from giving alms: He is more concerned about holding onto his wealth than about the greater blessing that he would receive for giving charity.

18. סוֹפֵג אֶת הַכֹּל — *Absorbs everything.* Though he remembers everything, he is not capable of distinguishing between the true and the false, the meaningful and the trivial.

מַשְׁפֵּךְ — *A funnel.* Everything passes through; he retains none of his studies and forgets everything he learns.

שְׁמוֹצִיאָה אֶת הַיַּיִן — *Which lets the wine flow through.* He retains only the minor, trivial points and forgets the major, basic points.

שְׁמוֹצִיאָה אֶת הַקֶּמַח — *Which allows the flour dust to pass through and retains the fine flour.* The ideal is a sieve which is so constructed that it lets the coarse grain pass through and retains in a receptacle

ה [יט] כָּל אַהֲבָה שֶׁהִיא תְלוּיָה בְדָבָר, בָּטֵל דָּבָר, בְּטֵלָה אַהֲבָה; וְשֶׁאֵינָהּ תְּלוּיָה בְדָבָר, אֵינָהּ בְּטֵלָה לְעוֹלָם. אֵיזוֹ הִיא אַהֲבָה שֶׁהִיא תְלוּיָה בְדָבָר? זוֹ אַהֲבַת אַמְנוֹן וְתָמָר. וְשֶׁאֵינָהּ תְּלוּיָה בְדָבָר? זוֹ אַהֲבַת דָּוִד וִיהוֹנָתָן.

[כ] כָּל מַחֲלֹקֶת שֶׁהִיא לְשֵׁם שָׁמַיִם, סוֹפָהּ לְהִתְקַיֵּם; וְשֶׁאֵינָהּ לְשֵׁם שָׁמַיִם, אֵין סוֹפָהּ לְהִתְקַיֵּם. אֵיזוֹ הִיא מַחֲלֹקֶת שֶׁהִיא לְשֵׁם שָׁמַיִם? זוֹ מַחֲלֹקֶת הִלֵּל וְשַׁמַּאי. וְשֶׁאֵינָהּ לְשֵׁם שָׁמַיִם? זוֹ מַחֲלֹקֶת קֹרַח וְכָל עֲדָתוֹ.

[כא] כָּל הַמְזַכֶּה אֶת הָרַבִּים, אֵין חֵטְא בָּא עַל יָדוֹ, וְכָל הַמַּחֲטִיא אֶת הָרַבִּים, אֵין מַסְפִּיקִין בְּיָדוֹ לַעֲשׂוֹת תְּשׁוּבָה. מֹשֶׁה זָכָה וְזִכָּה אֶת הָרַבִּים, זְכוּת הָרַבִּים תָּלוּי בּוֹ, שֶׁנֶּאֱמַר: "צִדְקַת יהוה עָשָׂה, וּמִשְׁפָּטָיו עִם יִשְׂרָאֵל". יָרָבְעָם בֶּן נְבָט חָטָא וְהֶחֱטִיא אֶת הָרַבִּים, חֵטְא הָרַבִּים תָּלוּי בּוֹ, שֶׁנֶּאֱמַר: "עַל חַטֹּאות יָרָבְעָם אֲשֶׁר חָטָא, וַאֲשֶׁר הֶחֱטִיא אֶת יִשְׂרָאֵל".

[כב] כָּל מִי שֶׁיֵּשׁ בְּיָדוֹ שְׁלֹשָׁה דְבָרִים הַלָּלוּ, הוּא מִתַּלְמִידָיו שֶׁל אַבְרָהָם אָבִינוּ; וּשְׁלֹשָׁה דְבָרִים אֲחֵרִים, הוּא מִתַּלְמִידָיו שֶׁל בִּלְעָם הָרָשָׁע. עַיִן טוֹבָה, וְרוּחַ נְמוּכָה, וְנֶפֶשׁ שְׁפָלָה — תַּלְמִידָיו שֶׁל אַבְרָהָם אָבִינוּ. עַיִן רָעָה, וְרוּחַ גְּבוֹהָה, וְנֶפֶשׁ רְחָבָה — תַּלְמִידָיו שֶׁל בִּלְעָם הָרָשָׁע. מַה בֵּין תַּלְמִידָיו שֶׁל אַבְרָהָם אָבִינוּ לְתַלְמִידָיו שֶׁל בִּלְעָם הָרָשָׁע? תַּלְמִידָיו שֶׁל אַבְרָהָם אָבִינוּ אוֹכְלִין בָּעוֹלָם הַזֶּה, וְנוֹחֲלִין הָעוֹלָם הַבָּא, שֶׁנֶּאֱמַר: "לְהַנְחִיל אֹהֲבַי יֵשׁ, וְאֹצְרֹתֵיהֶם אֲמַלֵּא". אֲבָל תַּלְמִידָיו שֶׁל בִּלְעָם הָרָשָׁע יוֹרְשִׁין גֵּיהִנֹּם, וְיוֹרְדִין לִבְאֵר שַׁחַת, שֶׁנֶּאֱמַר:

only the fine flour. The reference is to a student who retains the essence of his studies and ignores the superfluous.

19. שֶׁהִיא תְלוּיָה בְדָבָר — *That depends on a specific cause,* i.e., something material or sensual such as wealth or beauty, rather than an unselfish union based on mutual respect and affection, and an interest in the good of the person loved. אַמְנוֹן וְתָמָר — *Amnon for Tamar.* Amnon's love was motivated by Tamar's beauty. See *II Samuel* 13.

דָּוִד וִיהוֹנָתָן — *David and Jonathan,* whose souls were bound up with each other. Even though each knew that the other stood in the way of his succession to the throne, their love for each other was not affected. See *I Samuel* 18.

20. סוֹפָהּ לְהִתְקַיֵּם — *Will have a constructive outcome.* There are several interpretations: Their respective views will be remembered, even those of the one whose opinion is not adopted (*Rambam*); since their disputes result in

5 [19] *Any love that depends on a specific cause, when that cause is gone, the love is gone; but if it does not depend on a specific cause, it will never cease. What sort of love depended upon a specific cause? — The love of Amnon for Tamar. And what did not depend upon a specific cause? — The love of David and Jonathan.*

[20] *Any dispute that is for the sake of Heaven will have a constructive outcome; but one that is not for the sake of Heaven will not have a constructive outcome. What sort of dispute was for the sake of Heaven? — The dispute between Hillel and Shammai. And which was not for the sake of Heaven? — The dispute of Korah and his entire company.*

[21] *Whoever influences the masses to become meritorious shall not be the cause of sin; but one who influences the masses to sin will not be given the means to repent. Moses was meritorious and influenced the masses to be meritorious, so the merit of the masses was to his credit, as it is said: "He performed the righteousness of H*ASHEM*, and His laws together with Israel" (Deuteronomy 33:21). Jeroboam ben Nebat sinned and caused the masses to sin, so the sin of the masses is charged against him, as it is said: "For the sins of Jeroboam which he committed and which he caused Israel to commit" (I Kings 15:30)*

[22] *Whoever has the following three traits is among the disciples of our forefather Abraham; and [whoever has] three different traits is among the disciples of the wicked Balaam. Those who have a good eye, a humble spirit, and a meek soul are among the disciples of our forefather Abraham. Those who have an evil eye, an arrogant spirit, and a greedy soul are among the disciples of the wicked Balaam. How are the disciples of our forefather Abraham different from the disciples of the wicked Balaam? The disciples of our forefather Abraham enjoy [the fruits of their good deeds] in This World and inherit the World to Come, as is said: "To cause those who love Me to inherit an everlasting possession [the World to Come], and I will fill their storehouses [in This World]" (Proverbs 8:21). But the disciples of the wicked Balaam inherit Gehinnom and descend into the well of destruction, as is said:*

a clearer understanding of the Torah, they will continue to have such disputes (*R' Yonah*); the disputants will live and survive, unlike Korah's company that perished (*Rav*); the disputants will succeed in their goal of finding and clarifying the truth (*Rav*).

הִלֵּל וְשַׁמַּאי — *Hillel and Shammai.* Though they had disputes regarding Halachah, they were concerned not with triumph but with a sincere search for truth in the exposition of Torah.

קֹרַח וְכָל עֲדָתוֹ — *Korah and his entire company.* Their dispute was merely a rebellion against authority, and accordingly met a tragic end. See Numbers 16.

21. אֵין מַסְפִּיקִין בְּיָדוֹ לַעֲשׂוֹת תְּשׁוּבָה — *Will not be given the means to repent.* As a general rule, God helps those who seek to repent. But in the case of someone who is responsible for the spiritual downfall of others, it would be unfair to help him escape punishment while his victims must suffer for their sins.

ה „וְאַתָּה אֱלֹהִים תּוֹרִדֵם לִבְאֵר שַׁחַת, אַנְשֵׁי דָמִים וּמִרְמָה לֹא יֶחֱצוּ יְמֵיהֶם, וַאֲנִי אֶבְטַח בָּךְ״.

[כג] יְהוּדָה בֶּן תֵּימָא אוֹמֵר: הֱוֵי עַז כַּנָּמֵר, וְקַל כַּנֶּשֶׁר, רָץ כַּצְּבִי, וְגִבּוֹר כָּאֲרִי — לַעֲשׂוֹת רְצוֹן אָבִיךָ שֶׁבַּשָּׁמָיִם.

[כד] הוּא הָיָה אוֹמֵר: עַז פָּנִים לְגֵיהִנֹּם, וּבֹשֶׁת פָּנִים לְגַן עֵדֶן. יְהִי רָצוֹן מִלְּפָנֶיךָ, יהוה אֱלֹהֵינוּ וֵאלֹהֵי אֲבוֹתֵינוּ, שֶׁיִּבָּנֶה בֵּית הַמִּקְדָּשׁ בִּמְהֵרָה בְיָמֵינוּ, וְתֵן חֶלְקֵנוּ בְּתוֹרָתֶךָ.

[כה] הוּא הָיָה אוֹמֵר: בֶּן חָמֵשׁ שָׁנִים לַמִּקְרָא, בֶּן עֶשֶׂר שָׁנִים לַמִּשְׁנָה, בֶּן שְׁלֹשׁ עֶשְׂרֵה לַמִּצְוֹת, בֶּן חֲמֵשׁ עֶשְׂרֵה לַגְּמָרָא, בֶּן שְׁמוֹנֶה עֶשְׂרֵה לַחֻפָּה, בֶּן עֶשְׂרִים לִרְדּוֹף, בֶּן שְׁלֹשִׁים לַכֹּחַ, בֶּן אַרְבָּעִים לַבִּינָה, בֶּן חֲמִשִּׁים לָעֵצָה, בֶּן שִׁשִּׁים לְזִקְנָה, בֶּן שִׁבְעִים לְשֵׂיבָה, בֶּן שְׁמוֹנִים לִגְבוּרָה, בֶּן תִּשְׁעִים לָשׁוּחַ, בֶּן מֵאָה כְּאִלּוּ מֵת וְעָבַר וּבָטֵל מִן הָעוֹלָם.

[כו] בֶּן בַּג בַּג אוֹמֵר: הֲפָךְ בָּהּ וַהֲפָךְ בָּהּ, דְּכֹלָּא בָהּ; וּבָהּ תֶּחֱזֵי, וְסִיב וּבְלֵה בָהּ, וּמִנַּהּ לָא תָזוּעַ, שֶׁאֵין לְךָ מִדָּה טוֹבָה הֵימֶנָּה. בֶּן הֵא הֵא אוֹמֵר: לְפוּם צַעֲרָא אַגְרָא.

However, even so egregious a sinner *can* repent, though he will not receive Divine assistance.

24. וּבֹשֶׁת פָּנִים — *But the shamefaced*, i.e., those who feel a sense of shame when thinking about sin. Such people will not sin habitually and will be rewarded with Gan Eden.

יְהִי רָצוֹן מִלְּפָנֶיךָ — *May it be Your will.* According to the Vilna Gaon, this prayer belongs at the end of the chapter.

25. בֶּן עֶשְׂרִים לִרְדּוֹף — *A twenty-year-old begins pursuit [of a livelihood].* Most familiarly understood to refer to the pursuit of a livelihood, which naturally follows soon after marriage. Rashi cites an opinion that it refers to the age when the Heavenly court *pursues* man for his actions — holding him liable for Divine punishment for his sins.

בֶּן חֲמִשִּׁים לָעֵצָה — *A fifty-year-old can offer counsel.* Fifty was the age at which Levites were no longer considered fit for heavy work, but continued to act as guides and counselors to the younger Levites (*Numbers* 8:25). At this age one can draw on his life experience and intellect to advise others.

בֶּן שִׁשִּׁים לְזִקְנָה — *A sixty-year-old attains seniority* [literally, *old age*]. This denotes one's appearance at that age, or it refers to intellectual maturity (זָקֵן = זֶה שֶׁקָּנָה חָכְמָה).

בֶּן שִׁבְעִים לְשֵׂיבָה — *A seventy-year-old attains a ripe old age.* This was the age at which David died, of whom it was said: *he died in fullness of years* (בְּשֵׂיבָה טוֹבָה) (I *Chronicles* 29:28).

בֶּן שְׁמוֹנִים לִגְבוּרָה — *An eighty-year-old shows strength.* This follows *Psalms* 90:10: *The days of our years — among them are seventy years, and if with strength — eighty years.* When one lives to be over eighty, it is because God has granted him special natural strength and vigor; it is an age invested with an

5 *"And You, O God, shall lower them into the well of destruction, men of bloodshed and deceit shall not live out half their days; but as for me, I will trust in You"* (Psalms 55:24).

[23] **Yehudah ben Tema says: Be bold as a leopard, light as an eagle, swift as a deer, and strong as a lion, to carry out the will of your Father in Heaven.**

[24] **He used to say: The brazen goes to Gehinnom, but the shamefaced goes to the Garden of Eden. May it be Your will, HASHEM, our God and the God of our forefathers, that the Holy Temple be rebuilt, speedily in our days, and grant us our share in Your Torah.**

[25] **He used to say: A five-year-old begins Scripture; a ten-year-old begins Mishnah; a thirteen-year-old becomes obliged to observe the commandments; a fifteen-year-old begins the study of Gemara; an eighteen-year-old goes to the marriage canopy; a twenty-year-old begins pursuit [of a livelihood]; a thirty-year-old attains full strength; a forty-year-old attains understanding; a fifty-year-old can offer counsel; a sixty-year-old attains seniority; a seventy-year-old attains a ripe old age; an eighty-year-old shows strength; a ninety-year-old becomes stooped over; a hundred-year-old is as if he were dead, passed away, and ceased from the world.**

[26] **Ben Bag Bag says: Delve in it [the Torah] and continue to delve in it [the Torah] for everything is in it; look deeply into it; grow old and gray over it, and do not stir from it, for you can have no better portion than it. Ben Hei Hei says: The reward is in proportion to the exertion.**

abundance of spiritual vigor as well.

בֶּן מֵאָה כְּאִלּוּ מֵת — *A hundred-year-old is as if he were dead.* He has lost most of his natural faculties.

26. בֶּן בַּג בַּג ... בֶּן הֵא הֵא — *Ben Bag Bag ... Ben Hei Hei.* The former's full name was R' Yochanan ben Bag Bag (*Kiddushin* 10b). Both Bag Bag and Hei Hei were descendants of proselytes whose names were disguised to protect them from informers who would have turned them over to the Romans. Some interpret בֶּן בַּג בַּג as an abbreviation for בֶּן גֵּר בַּת גִּיּוֹרֶת, the son of male and female proselytes. There is a view that the name *Hei Hei* alludes to the first "proselytes," Abraham and Sarah, to each of whose names God added the letter ה, *hei*. Thus the name אַבְרָם became אַבְרָהָם and שָׂרַי became שָׂרָה. The name *Bag Bag* also contains this allusion because the numerical value of בַּג (2 and 3) equals ה (5). See *Tosafos Chagigah* 9b.

הֲפָךְ בָּהּ — *Delve in it* [the Torah; lit., *turn over in it*]. Study the Torah from all sides.

דְּכֹלָּא בָהּ — *For everything is in it.* The Torah is a self-contained guide to life; all of the world's wisdom is contained in it.

This and the following paragraph are quoted in Aramaic, the vernacular of Mishnaic times, since they were popular folk-sayings.

לְפוּם צַעֲרָא אַגְרָא — *The reward is in proportion to the exertion.* The reward for observing God's commandment is increased in proportion to the effort and discomfort one experiences in its performance.

ה

רַבִּי חֲנַנְיָא בֶּן עֲקַשְׁיָא אוֹמֵר: רָצָה הַקָּדוֹשׁ בָּרוּךְ הוּא לְזַכּוֹת אֶת יִשְׂרָאֵל, לְפִיכָךְ הִרְבָּה לָהֶם תּוֹרָה וּמִצְוֹת, שֶׁנֶּאֱמַר: "יהוה חָפֵץ לְמַעַן צִדְקוֹ, יַגְדִּיל תּוֹרָה וְיַאְדִּיר".

פרק ששי

ו

כָּל יִשְׂרָאֵל יֵשׁ לָהֶם חֵלֶק לָעוֹלָם הַבָּא, שֶׁנֶּאֱמַר: "וְעַמֵּךְ כֻּלָּם צַדִּיקִים, לְעוֹלָם יִירְשׁוּ אָרֶץ, נֵצֶר מַטָּעַי, מַעֲשֵׂה יָדַי לְהִתְפָּאֵר".

שָׁנוּ חֲכָמִים בִּלְשׁוֹן הַמִּשְׁנָה. בָּרוּךְ שֶׁבָּחַר בָּהֶם וּבְמִשְׁנָתָם.

[א] רַבִּי מֵאִיר אוֹמֵר: כָּל הָעוֹסֵק בַּתּוֹרָה לִשְׁמָהּ זוֹכֶה לִדְבָרִים הַרְבֵּה; וְלֹא עוֹד, אֶלָּא שֶׁכָּל הָעוֹלָם כֻּלּוֹ כְּדַאי הוּא לוֹ. נִקְרָא רֵעַ, אָהוּב. אוֹהֵב אֶת הַמָּקוֹם, אוֹהֵב אֶת הַבְּרִיּוֹת, מְשַׂמֵּחַ אֶת הַמָּקוֹם, מְשַׂמֵּחַ אֶת הַבְּרִיּוֹת. וּמַלְבַּשְׁתּוֹ עֲנָוָה וְיִרְאָה; וּמַכְשַׁרְתּוֹ לִהְיוֹת צַדִּיק, חָסִיד, יָשָׁר, וְנֶאֱמָן; וּמְרַחַקְתּוֹ מִן הַחֵטְא, וּמְקָרַבְתּוֹ לִידֵי זְכוּת. וְנֶהֱנִין מִמֶּנּוּ עֵצָה וְתוּשִׁיָּה, בִּינָה וּגְבוּרָה, שֶׁנֶּאֱמַר: "לִי עֵצָה וְתוּשִׁיָּה, אֲנִי בִינָה, לִי גְבוּרָה". וְנוֹתֶנֶת לוֹ מַלְכוּת, וּמֶמְשָׁלָה, וְחִקּוּר דִּין; וּמְגַלִּין לוֹ רָזֵי תוֹרָה; וְנַעֲשֶׂה כְּמַעְיָן הַמִּתְגַּבֵּר, וּכְנָהָר שֶׁאֵינוֹ פוֹסֵק; וְהֹוֶה צָנוּעַ, וְאֶרֶךְ רוּחַ, וּמוֹחֵל עַל עֶלְבּוֹנוֹ. וּמְגַדַּלְתּוֹ וּמְרוֹמַמְתּוֹ עַל כָּל הַמַּעֲשִׂים.

CHAPTER SIX

שָׁנוּ חֲכָמִים — *The Sages taught.* This phrase is the Hebrew equivalent of the familiar Aramaic תָּנוּ רַבָּנָן which the Talmud uses to introduce a *baraisa*. The word *baraisa*, literally *outside*, refers to Tannaitic teachings that were not selected for inclusion in the Mishnah, but were preserved "outside" of it. They were written in the style of the Mishnah and supplement it.

This chapter is not part of Tractate *Avos*, but is a collection of *baraisos* (*Kallah* 8). Its inclusion brings to six the number of chapters in *Pirkei Avos*, corresponding to the six Sabbaths between Pesach and Shavuos, during which one cycle of *Pirkei Avos* is read, one chapter each Sabbath. Thus, this chapter is studied on the Sabbath preceding Shavuos, the Festival commemorating the giving of the Torah. Dealing as it does with acquiring Torah knowledge, this final added chapter has been named קִנְיַן תּוֹרָה, *Acquisition of Torah*. It is also called *Baraisa of R' Meir* since it opens with a *baraisa* attributed to him.

1. On the qualities acquired from Torah study.

5

Rabbi Chanania ben Akashia says: The Holy One, Blessed is He, wished to confer merit upon Israel; therefore He gave them Torah and mitzvos in abundance, as it is said: "HASHEM desired, for the sake of its [Israel's] righteousness, that the Torah be made great and glorious" (Isaiah 42:21).

6

⊰ CHAPTER SIX ⊱

All Israel has a share in the World to Come, as it is said: "And your people are all righteous; they shall inherit the land forever; they are the branch of My planting, My handiwork, in which to take pride" (Isaiah 60:21).

שָׁנוּ חֲכָמִים *The Sages taught [this chapter] in the language of the Mishnah. Blessed is He Who chose them and their teaching.*

[1] Rabbi Meir says: Whoever engages in Torah study for its own sake merits many things; furthermore, [the creation of] the entire world is worthwhile for his sake alone. He is called, "Friend, Beloved." He loves the Omnipresent, he loves [His] creatures, he gladdens the Omnipresent, he gladdens [His] creatures. [The Torah] clothes him in humility and fear [of God]; it makes him fit to be righteous, devout, fair, and faithful. It moves him away from sin and draws him near to merit. From him people enjoy counsel and wisdom, understanding and strength, as it is said: "Mine are counsel and wisdom, I am understanding, mine is strength"(Proverbs 8:14). [The Torah] gives him kingship and dominion and analytical judgment; the secrets of the Torah are revealed to him; he becomes like a steadily strengthening fountain and like an unceasing river. He becomes modest, patient, and forgiving of insult to himself. [The Torah] makes him great and exalts him above all things.

לשְׁמָהּ — **For its own sake.** From pure love of God, and for the sole motive of acquiring a knowledge of God's will, and fulfilling His commandments without any ulterior motive.

וזוֹכֶה לִדְבָרִים הַרְבֵּה — **Merits many things.** The blessings awaiting this person are too bountiful to be specified.

כְּדַאי הוּא לוֹ — **Is worthwhile for his sake alone.** The entire world was created for such a person since its purpose is realized through him.

אוֹהֵב אֶת הַבְּרִיוֹת — **He loves [His] creatures,** without distinction, cynicism, or malice of any kind, because they are God's creation.

לִי עֵצָה וְתוּשִׁיָּה — **Mine are counsel and wisdom.** The "speaker" is the Torah. It tells its adherents that it provides not only wisdom, but the spiritual *strength* to prevail over adversity. Furthermore it gives kings and scholars the guidance in law and behavior to exercise moral power.

[ב] אָמַר רַבִּי יְהוֹשֻׁעַ בֶּן לֵוִי: בְּכָל יוֹם וָיוֹם בַּת קוֹל יוֹצֵאת מֵהַר חוֹרֵב, וּמַכְרֶזֶת וְאוֹמֶרֶת: "אוֹי לָהֶם לַבְּרִיּוֹת, מֵעֶלְבּוֹנָהּ שֶׁל תּוֹרָה!", שֶׁכָּל מִי שֶׁאֵינוֹ עוֹסֵק בַּתּוֹרָה נִקְרָא נָזוּף, שֶׁנֶּאֱמַר: "נֶזֶם זָהָב בְּאַף חֲזִיר, אִשָּׁה יָפָה וְסָרַת טָעַם". וְאוֹמֵר: "וְהַלֻּחֹת מַעֲשֵׂה אֱלֹהִים הֵמָּה, וְהַמִּכְתָּב מִכְתַּב אֱלֹהִים הוּא חָרוּת עַל הַלֻּחֹת". אַל תִּקְרָא "חָרוּת" אֶלָּא "חֵרוּת", שֶׁאֵין לְךָ בֶּן חוֹרִין אֶלָּא מִי שֶׁעוֹסֵק בְּתַלְמוּד תּוֹרָה. וְכָל מִי שֶׁעוֹסֵק בְּתַלְמוּד תּוֹרָה הֲרֵי זֶה מִתְעַלֶּה, שֶׁנֶּאֱמַר: "וּמִמַּתָּנָה נַחֲלִיאֵל, וּמִנַּחֲלִיאֵל בָּמוֹת".

[ג] הַלּוֹמֵד מֵחֲבֵרוֹ פֶּרֶק אֶחָד, אוֹ הֲלָכָה אַחַת, אוֹ פָּסוּק אֶחָד, אוֹ דִּבּוּר אֶחָד, אוֹ אֲפִילוּ אוֹת אַחַת — צָרִיךְ לִנְהָג בּוֹ כָּבוֹד. שֶׁכֵּן מָצִינוּ בְּדָוִד מֶלֶךְ יִשְׂרָאֵל, שֶׁלֹּא לָמַד מֵאֲחִיתֹפֶל אֶלָּא שְׁנֵי דְבָרִים בִּלְבַד, וּקְרָאוֹ רַבּוֹ, אַלּוּפוֹ, וּמְיֻדָּעוֹ, שֶׁנֶּאֱמַר: "וְאַתָּה אֱנוֹשׁ כְּעֶרְכִּי, אַלּוּפִי וּמְיֻדָּעִי". וַהֲלֹא דְבָרִים קַל וָחֹמֶר: וּמַה דָּוִד מֶלֶךְ יִשְׂרָאֵל, שֶׁלֹּא לָמַד מֵאֲחִיתֹפֶל אֶלָּא שְׁנֵי דְבָרִים בִּלְבַד, קְרָאוֹ רַבּוֹ אַלּוּפוֹ וּמְיֻדָּעוֹ — הַלּוֹמֵד מֵחֲבֵרוֹ פֶּרֶק אֶחָד, אוֹ הֲלָכָה אַחַת, אוֹ פָּסוּק אֶחָד, אוֹ דִּבּוּר אֶחָד, אוֹ אֲפִילוּ אוֹת אַחַת, עַל אַחַת כַּמָּה וְכַמָּה שֶׁצָּרִיךְ לִנְהָג בּוֹ כָּבוֹד! וְאֵין כָּבוֹד אֶלָּא תוֹרָה, שֶׁנֶּאֱמַר: "כָּבוֹד חֲכָמִים יִנְחָלוּ", "וּתְמִימִים יִנְחֲלוּ טוֹב", וְאֵין טוֹב אֶלָּא תוֹרָה, שֶׁנֶּאֱמַר: "כִּי לֶקַח טוֹב נָתַתִּי לָכֶם, תּוֹרָתִי אַל תַּעֲזֹבוּ".

[ד] כָּךְ הִיא דַּרְכָּהּ שֶׁל תּוֹרָה: פַּת בְּמֶלַח תֹּאכַל, וּמַיִם בִּמְשׂוּרָה תִּשְׁתֶּה, וְעַל הָאָרֶץ תִּישָׁן, וְחַיֵּי צַעַר תִּחְיֶה, וּבַתּוֹרָה אַתָּה עָמֵל; אִם אַתָּה עוֹשֶׂה כֵּן, "אַשְׁרֶיךָ וְטוֹב לָךְ". "אַשְׁרֶיךָ" — בָּעוֹלָם הַזֶּה, "וְטוֹב לָךְ" — לָעוֹלָם הַבָּא.

2. מֵהַר חוֹרֵב — *From Mount Horeb.* Another name for Mount Sinai, where the Torah was given. This voice from Mount Horeb denotes the perpetual witness of the Torah to man's actions.

נֶזֶם זָהָב בְּאַף חֲזִיר — *Like a golden ring in a swine's snout.* In our context the Torah is represented by a golden ring which becomes degraded and sullied when the "pig" wallows in dirt. This proof verse is related by means of the Rabbinic exposition of *notarikon* (abbreviated shorthand), whereby the initial letters of נֶזֶם נָזוּף are combined with the last letter of בְּאַף to form נָזוּף.

וְאוֹמֵר — *And it says:* The *baraisa* now teaches another lesson regarding those who are committed to Torah: It is the source of true freedom.

אַל תִּקְרָא "חָרוּת" אֶלָּא "חֵרוּת" — *Do not read "charus" (engraved) but "cherus" (freedom).* The Torah is unvowelized,

6 [2] *Rabbi Yehoshua ben Levi said: Every single day a Heavenly voice emanates from Mount Horeb, proclaiming and saying, "Woe to them, to the people, because of [their] insult to the Torah!" For whoever does not occupy himself with the Torah is called, "Rebuked," as it is said: "Like a golden ring in a swine's snout is a beautiful woman who turns away from good judgment" (Proverbs 11:22). And it says: "The Tablets are God's handiwork and the script was God's script charus (engraved) on the Tablets" (Exodus 32:16). Do not read "charus" (engraved) but "cherus" (freedom), for you can have no freer man than one who engages in the study of the Torah. And anyone who engages in the study of the Torah becomes elevated, as it is said: "From Mattanah to Nachaliel, and from Nachaliel to Bamos" (Numbers 21:19).*

[3] *He who learns from his fellowman a single chapter, a single halachah, a single verse, a single Torah statement, or even a single letter, must treat him with honor. For thus we find in the case of David, king of Israel, who learned nothing from Achitophel except for two things, yet called him his teacher, his guide, his intimate, as it is said: "You are a man of my measure, my guide and my intimate" (Psalms 55:14). One can derive from this the following: If David, king of Israel, who learned nothing from Achitophel except for two things, called him his teacher, his guide, his intimate — one who learns from his fellowman a single chapter, a single halachah, a single verse, a single statement, or even a single letter, how much more must he treat him with honor! And honor is due only for Torah, as it is said: "The wise shall inherit honor" (Proverbs 3:35). "... and the perfect shall inherit good" (ibid. 28:10). And only Torah is truly good, as it is said: "I have given you a good teaching, do not forsake My Torah" (ibid. 4:2).*

[4] *This is the way of Torah: Eat bread with salt, drink water in small measure, sleep on the ground, live a life of deprivation — but toil in the Torah! If you do this, "You are praiseworthy, and all is well with you" (Psalms 128:2). "You are praiseworthy" — in This World; "and all is well with you" — in the World to Come.*

and the Rabbis often employ this interpretive method of reading a word with different vowels to elicit a homiletic thought. Nevertheless, the simple meaning of the verse remains unchanged.

וּמִמַּתָּנָה ... נַחֲלִיאֵל ... בָּמוֹת — *Mattanah ... Nachaliel ... Bamos.* These are place names which are homiletically interpreted here in their literal sense — מַתָּנָה, *gift* ... נַחֲלִיאֵל, *Divine heritage* ... בָּמוֹת, *heights* — rendering the verse: *From the gift of Torah man gains a Divine heritage which elevates him and leads him to lofty spiritual heights.*

3. שְׁנֵי דְבָרִים — *Two things.* They were: that one should not study Torah alone but with a colleague; and that when going to the House of God one should walk with reverence — or according to another interpretation: run with exuberance and vigor.

4. כָּךְ הִיא דַרְכָּהּ — *This is the way.* Asceticism is not being advocated here; one

ו [ה] אַל תְּבַקֵּשׁ גְּדֻלָּה לְעַצְמְךָ, וְאַל תַּחְמֹד כָּבוֹד; יוֹתֵר מִלִּמּוּדְךָ עֲשֵׂה. וְאַל תִּתְאַוֶּה לְשֻׁלְחָנָם שֶׁל מְלָכִים, שֶׁשֻּׁלְחָנְךָ גָּדוֹל מִשֻּׁלְחָנָם, וְכִתְרְךָ גָּדוֹל מִכִּתְרָם; וְנֶאֱמָן הוּא בַּעַל מְלַאכְתְּךָ, שֶׁיְּשַׁלֶּם לְךָ שְׂכַר פְּעֻלָּתֶךָ.

[ו] גְּדוֹלָה תוֹרָה יוֹתֵר מִן הַכְּהֻנָּה וּמִן הַמַּלְכוּת, שֶׁהַמַּלְכוּת נִקְנֵית בִּשְׁלֹשִׁים מַעֲלוֹת, וְהַכְּהֻנָּה נִקְנֵית בְּעֶשְׂרִים וְאַרְבָּעָה, וְהַתּוֹרָה נִקְנֵית בְּאַרְבָּעִים וּשְׁמוֹנָה דְבָרִים, וְאֵלּוּ הֵן: בְּתַלְמוּד, בִּשְׁמִיעַת הָאֹזֶן, בַּעֲרִיכַת שְׂפָתַיִם, בְּבִינַת הַלֵּב, בְּשִׂכְלוּת הַלֵּב, בְּאֵימָה, בְּיִרְאָה, בַּעֲנָוָה, בְּשִׂמְחָה, בְּטָהֳרָה, בְּשִׁמּוּשׁ חֲכָמִים, בְּדִקְדּוּק חֲבֵרִים, בְּפִלְפּוּל הַתַּלְמִידִים, בְּיִשּׁוּב, בְּמִקְרָא, בְּמִשְׁנָה, בְּמִעוּט סְחוֹרָה, בְּמִעוּט דֶּרֶךְ אֶרֶץ, בְּמִעוּט תַּעֲנוּג, בְּמִעוּט שֵׁנָה, בְּמִעוּט שִׂיחָה, בְּמִעוּט שְׂחוֹק, בְּאֶרֶךְ אַפַּיִם, בְּלֵב טוֹב, בֶּאֱמוּנַת חֲכָמִים, בְּקַבָּלַת הַיִּסּוּרִין, הַמַּכִּיר אֶת מְקוֹמוֹ, וְהַשָּׂמֵחַ בְּחֶלְקוֹ, וְהָעוֹשֶׂה סְיָג לִדְבָרָיו, וְאֵינוֹ מַחֲזִיק טוֹבָה לְעַצְמוֹ, אָהוּב, אוֹהֵב אֶת הַמָּקוֹם, אוֹהֵב אֶת הַבְּרִיּוֹת, אוֹהֵב אֶת הַצְּדָקוֹת, אוֹהֵב אֶת הַמֵּישָׁרִים, אוֹהֵב אֶת הַתּוֹכָחוֹת, וּמִתְרַחֵק מִן הַכָּבוֹד, וְלֹא מֵגִיס לִבּוֹ בְּתַלְמוּדוֹ, וְאֵינוֹ שָׂמֵחַ בְּהוֹרָאָה, נוֹשֵׂא בְעֹל עִם חֲבֵרוֹ, וּמַכְרִיעוֹ לְכַף זְכוּת, וּמַעֲמִידוֹ עַל הָאֱמֶת, וּמַעֲמִידוֹ עַל הַשָּׁלוֹם, וּמִתְיַשֵּׁב לִבּוֹ בְּתַלְמוּדוֹ, שׁוֹאֵל וּמֵשִׁיב, שׁוֹמֵעַ וּמוֹסִיף, הַלּוֹמֵד עַל מְנָת לְלַמֵּד, וְהַלּוֹמֵד עַל מְנָת לַעֲשׂוֹת, הַמַּחְכִּים אֶת רַבּוֹ, וְהַמְכַוֵּן אֶת שְׁמוּעָתוֹ, וְהָאוֹמֵר דָּבָר בְּשֵׁם אוֹמְרוֹ. הָא לָמַדְתָּ, כָּל הָאוֹמֵר דָּבָר בְּשֵׁם אוֹמְרוֹ, מֵבִיא גְאֻלָּה לָעוֹלָם, שֶׁנֶּאֱמַר: "וַתֹּאמֶר אֶסְתֵּר לַמֶּלֶךְ בְּשֵׁם מָרְדֳּכָי".

[ז] גְּדוֹלָה תוֹרָה, שֶׁהִיא נוֹתֶנֶת חַיִּים לְעוֹשֶׂיהָ בָּעוֹלָם הַזֶּה וּבָעוֹלָם הַבָּא, שֶׁנֶּאֱמַר: "כִּי חַיִּים הֵם לְמֹצְאֵיהֶם, וּלְכָל

who is wealthy is not expected to cast away his wealth in the pursuit of Torah. Rather, this is a general call for moderation and an address to the poor person: Even if you are poverty stricken, do not neglect Torah study to pursue tangible wealth. The serenity of Torah can be experienced even in privation, and one must always be prepared to sacrifice his personal comfort on behalf of Torah.

5. וְאַל תַּחְמֹד כָּבוֹד — *And do not crave honor* for your scholarly attainments in Torah study, for you will thereby negate the pure motives required for study of Torah for its own sake (see mishnah 1).

יוֹתֵר מִלִּמּוּדְךָ עֲשֵׂה — *Let your performance exceed your learning.* See 3:12.

6 [5] *Do not seek greatness for yourself, and do not crave honor; let your performance exceed your learning. Do not lust for the table of kings, for your table is greater than theirs, and your crown is greater than their crown; and your Employer is trustworthy to pay you remuneration for your deeds.*

[6] *Torah is even greater than priesthood or royalty; for royalty is acquired along with thirty prerogatives, and the priesthood with twenty-four [gifts], but the Torah is acquired by means of forty-eight qualities, which are: Study, attentive listening, articulate speech, intuitive understanding, discernment, awe, reverence, modesty, joy, purity, ministering to the Sages, closeness with colleagues, sharp discussion with students, deliberation, [knowledge of] Scripture, Mishnah, limited business activity, limited sexual activity, limited pleasure, limited sleep, limited conversation, limited laughter, slowness to anger, a good heart, faith in the Sages, acceptance of suffering, knowing one's place, being happy with one's lot, making a protective fence around his personal matters, claiming no credit for himself, being beloved, loving the Omnipresent, loving [His] creatures, loving righteous ways, loving justice, loving reproof, keeping far from honor, not being arrogant with his learning, not enjoying halachic decision-making, sharing his fellow's yoke, judging him favorably, setting him on the truthful course, setting him on the peaceful course, thinking deliberately in his study, asking and answering, listening and contributing to the discussion, learning in order to teach, learning in order to practice, making his teacher wiser, pondering over what he has learned, and repeating a saying in the name of the one who said it. For you have learned this: Whoever repeats a thing in the name of the one who said it brings redemption to the world, as it is said: "And Esther said to the king in the name of Mordechai" (Esther 2:22).*

[7] *Great is Torah, for it confers life upon its practitioners, both in This World and in the World to Come, as it is said: "For they [the*

שֻׁלְחָנְךָ — *For your table*, i.e., spiritually in the World to Come.

6. בִּשְׁלֹשִׁים מַעֲלוֹת — *Along with thirty prerogatives*. These are privileges that go with the office. They are enumerated in *Sanhedrin* 18a. See also *I Samuel* 8:11ff and *Deuteronomy* 17:5ff.

בְּעֶשְׂרִים וְאַרְבָּעָה — *With twenty-four [gifts]*. The twenty-four priestly gifts are deduced from *Leviticus* 21 and *Numbers* 18.

בֶּאֱמוּנַת חֲכָמִים — *Faith in the Sages*, i.e., in the authenticity of their teachings as representing the Oral Law transmitted to Moses at Sinai.

הַמַּחְכִּים אֶת רַבּוֹ — *Making his teacher wiser*, by sharpening his mind through asking incisive questions and seeking constant clarification of his teachings. Compare the Rabbinic maxim: "Much have I learned from my teachers, more from my colleagues, but most of all from my students" (*Taanis* 7a).

וְהָאוֹמֵר דָּבָר בְּשֵׁם אוֹמְרוֹ — *And repeating a saying in the name of the one who said it*, thus not falsely taking credit for someone else's statement. One must display indebtedness to a source and mention him by name. The mention of Mordechai's name in *Esther* 6:2 eventually led

בִּשְׂרוֹ מַרְפֵּא״. וְאוֹמֵר: ״רִפְאוּת תְּהִי לְשָׁרֶךָ, וְשִׁקּוּי לְעַצְמוֹתֶיךָ״. וְאוֹמֵר: ״עֵץ חַיִּים הִיא לַמַּחֲזִיקִים בָּהּ, וְתֹמְכֶיהָ מְאֻשָּׁר״. וְאוֹמֵר: ״כִּי לִוְיַת חֵן הֵם לְרֹאשֶׁךָ, וַעֲנָקִים לְגַרְגְּרֹתֶיךָ״. וְאוֹמֵר: ״תִּתֵּן לְרֹאשְׁךָ לִוְיַת חֵן, עֲטֶרֶת תִּפְאֶרֶת תְּמַגְּנֶךָּ״. וְאוֹמֵר: ״כִּי בִי יִרְבּוּ יָמֶיךָ, וְיוֹסִיפוּ לְךָ שְׁנוֹת חַיִּים״. וְאוֹמֵר: ״אֹרֶךְ יָמִים בִּימִינָהּ, בִּשְׂמֹאולָהּ עֹשֶׁר וְכָבוֹד״. וְאוֹמֵר: ״כִּי אֹרֶךְ יָמִים וּשְׁנוֹת חַיִּים, וְשָׁלוֹם יוֹסִיפוּ לָךְ״.

[ח] רַבִּי שִׁמְעוֹן בֶּן יְהוּדָה מִשּׁוּם רַבִּי שִׁמְעוֹן בֶּן יוֹחַאי אוֹמֵר: הַנּוֹי, וְהַכֹּחַ, וְהָעֹשֶׁר, וְהַכָּבוֹד, וְהַחָכְמָה, וְהַזִּקְנָה, וְהַשֵּׂיבָה, וְהַבָּנִים — נָאֶה לַצַּדִּיקִים וְנָאֶה לָעוֹלָם, שֶׁנֶּאֱמַר: ״עֲטֶרֶת תִּפְאֶרֶת שֵׂיבָה, בְּדֶרֶךְ צְדָקָה תִּמָּצֵא״. וְאוֹמֵר: ״עֲטֶרֶת זְקֵנִים בְּנֵי בָנִים, וְתִפְאֶרֶת בָּנִים אֲבוֹתָם״. וְאוֹמֵר: ״תִּפְאֶרֶת בַּחוּרִים כֹּחָם, וַהֲדַר זְקֵנִים שֵׂיבָה״. וְאוֹמֵר ״וְחָפְרָה הַלְּבָנָה וּבוֹשָׁה הַחַמָּה, כִּי מָלַךְ יהוה צְבָאוֹת בְּהַר צִיּוֹן וּבִירוּשָׁלַיִם, וְנֶגֶד זְקֵנָיו כָּבוֹד״. רַבִּי שִׁמְעוֹן בֶּן מְנַסְיָא אוֹמֵר: אֵלּוּ שֶׁבַע מִדּוֹת, שֶׁמָּנוּ חֲכָמִים לַצַּדִּיקִים, כֻּלָּם נִתְקַיְּמוּ בְּרַבִּי וּבְבָנָיו.

[ט] אָמַר רַבִּי יוֹסֵי בֶּן קִסְמָא: פַּעַם אַחַת הָיִיתִי מְהַלֵּךְ בַּדֶּרֶךְ, וּפָגַע בִּי אָדָם אֶחָד. וְנָתַן לִי שָׁלוֹם, וְהֶחֱזַרְתִּי לוֹ שָׁלוֹם. אָמַר לִי: ״רַבִּי, מֵאֵיזֶה מָקוֹם אָתָּה?״ אָמַרְתִּי לוֹ: ״מֵעִיר גְּדוֹלָה שֶׁל חֲכָמִים וְשֶׁל סוֹפְרִים אָנִי״. אָמַר לִי: ״רַבִּי, רְצוֹנְךָ שֶׁתָּדוּר עִמָּנוּ בִּמְקוֹמֵנוּ, וַאֲנִי אֶתֵּן לְךָ אֶלֶף אֲלָפִים דִּינְרֵי זָהָב וַאֲבָנִים טוֹבוֹת וּמַרְגָּלִיּוֹת?״ אָמַרְתִּי לוֹ: ״אִם אַתָּה נוֹתֵן לִי כָּל כֶּסֶף וְזָהָב וַאֲבָנִים טוֹבוֹת וּמַרְגָּלִיּוֹת שֶׁבָּעוֹלָם, אֵינִי דָר אֶלָּא בִּמְקוֹם תּוֹרָה״. וְכֵן כָּתוּב בְּסֵפֶר תְּהִלִּים עַל יְדֵי דָוִד מֶלֶךְ יִשְׂרָאֵל: ״טוֹב לִי תוֹרַת פִּיךָ מֵאַלְפֵי זָהָב וָכָסֶף״. וְלֹא עוֹד אֶלָּא שֶׁבִּשְׁעַת פְּטִירָתוֹ שֶׁל אָדָם אֵין מְלַוִּין לוֹ לְאָדָם לֹא כֶסֶף וְלֹא זָהָב וְלֹא אֲבָנִים טוֹבוֹת וּמַרְגָּלִיּוֹת, אֶלָּא תוֹרָה וּמַעֲשִׂים טוֹבִים בִּלְבָד, שֶׁנֶּאֱמַר: ״בְּהִתְהַלֶּכְךָ תַּנְחֶה אֹתָךְ, בְּשָׁכְבְּךָ תִּשְׁמֹר עָלֶיךָ, וַהֲקִיצוֹתָ הִיא תְשִׂיחֶךָ״. ״בְּהִתְהַלֶּכְךָ תַּנְחֶה אֹתָךְ״ — בָּעוֹלָם

---

to the miracle of Purim and the salvation of the Jews in Persia.

7. The Biblical verses in this *baraisa* are taken from *Proverbs*, where the subject is the wisdom of the Torah.

8. נָאֶה לַצַּדִּיקִים — *Befit the righteous.* They can be instruments for attaining righteousness or secular worldliness, depending upon how their possessor utilizes these adornments.

6 *teachings of the Torah] are life to those who find them, and a healing to his entire flesh"(Proverbs 4:22). And it says: "It shall be healing to your body, and marrow to your bones" (ibid. 3:8). And it says: "It is a tree of life to those who grasp it, and its supporters are praiseworthy" (ibid. 3:18) And it says: "They are a garland of grace for your head, and necklaces for your neck" (ibid. 1:9). And it says: "It will give to your head a garland of grace, a crown of glory it will deliver to you" (ibid. 4:9). And it says: "Indeed, through me [the Torah] your days shall be increased, and years of life shall be added to you" (ibid. 9:11). And it says: "Lengthy days are at its right, and at its left are wealth and honor" (ibid 3:16). And it says: "For lengthy days and years of life, and peace shall they add to you" (ibid. 3:2).*

[8] *Rabbi Shimon ben Yehudah says in the name of Rabbi Shimon ben Yochai: Beauty, strength, wealth, honor, wisdom, old age, hoary age, and children — these befit the righteous and befit the world, as it is said: "Ripe old age is a crown of splendor, it can be found in the path of righteousness" (ibid. 16:31). And it says: "The crown of the aged is grandchildren, and the splendor of children is their fathers" (ibid. 17:6) And it says: "The splendor of young men is their strength, and the glory of old men is hoary age" (ibid. 20:29) And it says: "The moon will grow pale and the sun be shamed, when HASHEM, Master of Legions, will have reigned on Mount Zion and in Jerusalem, and honor shall be before His elders" (Isaiah 24:23). Rabbi Shimon ben Menasya says: These seven qualities that the Sages attributed to the righteous were all realized in Rebbi and his sons.*

[9] *Rabbi Yose ben Kisma said: Once I was walking on the road, when a certain man met me. He greeted me and I returned his greeting. He said to me, "Rabbi, from what place are you?" I said to him, "I am from a great city of scholars and sages." He said to me, "Rabbi, would you be willing to live with us in our place? I would give you thousands upon thousands of golden dinars, precious stones, and pearls." I replied, "Even if you were to give me all the silver and gold, precious stones and pearls in the world, I would dwell nowhere but in a place of Torah." And so it is written in the Book of Psalms by David, King of Israel: "I prefer the Torah of Your mouth above thousands in gold and silver" (Psalms 119:72). Furthermore, when a man departs from This World, neither silver, nor gold, nor precious stones, nor pearls escort him, but only Torah study and good deeds, as it is said: "When you walk, it shall guide you; when you lie down, it shall guard you; and when you awake, it shall speak on your behalf" (Proverbs 6:22) "When you walk,*

שֶׁבַע — *Seven.* Actually *eight* adornments appear to be enumerated in this *baraisa.* The *Vilna Gaon* omits "wisdom," as it is not referred to in the proof texts cited, while the parallel dictum in *Yerushalmi Sanhedrin* 11:3 omits "old age."

בְּרַבִּי — *In Rebbi,* Rabbi Yehudah Ha-Nassi (the Prince). See 2:1.

ו הַזֶּה, "בְּשָׁכְבְּךָ תִּשְׁמֹר עָלֶיךָ" — בַּקֶּבֶר; "וַהֲקִיצוֹתָ הִיא תְשִׂיחֶךָ" — לָעוֹלָם הַבָּא. וְאוֹמֵר: "לִי הַכֶּסֶף וְלִי הַזָּהָב, נְאֻם יהוה צְבָאוֹת".

[י] חֲמִשָּׁה קִנְיָנִים קָנָה הַקָּדוֹשׁ בָּרוּךְ הוּא בְּעוֹלָמוֹ, וְאֵלּוּ הֵן: תּוֹרָה — קִנְיָן אֶחָד, שָׁמַיִם וָאָרֶץ — קִנְיָן אֶחָד, אַבְרָהָם — קִנְיָן אֶחָד, יִשְׂרָאֵל — קִנְיָן אֶחָד, בֵּית הַמִּקְדָּשׁ — קִנְיָן אֶחָד. תּוֹרָה מִנַּיִן? דִּכְתִיב: "יהוה קָנָנִי רֵאשִׁית דַּרְכּוֹ, קֶדֶם מִפְעָלָיו מֵאָז". שָׁמַיִם וָאָרֶץ מִנַּיִן? דִּכְתִיב: "כֹּה אָמַר יהוה, הַשָּׁמַיִם כִּסְאִי, וְהָאָרֶץ הֲדֹם רַגְלָי, אֵי זֶה בַיִת אֲשֶׁר תִּבְנוּ לִי, וְאֵי זֶה מָקוֹם מְנוּחָתִי"; וְאוֹמֵר: "מָה רַבּוּ מַעֲשֶׂיךָ יהוה, כֻּלָּם בְּחָכְמָה עָשִׂיתָ, מָלְאָה הָאָרֶץ קִנְיָנֶךָ". אַבְרָהָם מִנַּיִן? דִּכְתִיב: "וַיְבָרְכֵהוּ וַיֹּאמַר, בָּרוּךְ אַבְרָם לְאֵל עֶלְיוֹן, קֹנֵה שָׁמַיִם וָאָרֶץ". יִשְׂרָאֵל מִנַּיִן? דִּכְתִיב: "עַד יַעֲבֹר עַמְּךָ יהוה, עַד יַעֲבֹר עַם זוּ קָנִיתָ"; וְאוֹמֵר: "לִקְדוֹשִׁים אֲשֶׁר בָּאָרֶץ הֵמָּה, וְאַדִּירֵי כָּל חֶפְצִי בָם". בֵּית הַמִּקְדָּשׁ מִנַּיִן? דִּכְתִיב: "מָכוֹן לְשִׁבְתְּךָ פָּעַלְתָּ יהוה, מִקְּדָשׁ אֲדֹנָי כּוֹנְנוּ יָדֶיךָ"; וְאוֹמֵר: "וַיְבִיאֵם אֶל גְּבוּל קָדְשׁוֹ, הַר זֶה קָנְתָה יְמִינוֹ".

[יא] כָּל מַה שֶּׁבָּרָא הַקָּדוֹשׁ בָּרוּךְ הוּא בְּעוֹלָמוֹ לֹא בְרָאוֹ אֶלָּא לִכְבוֹדוֹ, שֶׁנֶּאֱמַר: "כֹּל הַנִּקְרָא בִשְׁמִי וְלִכְבוֹדִי בְּרָאתִיו, יְצַרְתִּיו אַף עֲשִׂיתִיו"; וְאוֹמֵר: "יהוה יִמְלֹךְ לְעֹלָם וָעֶד".

❧ ❧ ❧

רַבִּי חֲנַנְיָא בֶּן עֲקַשְׁיָא אוֹמֵר: רָצָה הַקָּדוֹשׁ בָּרוּךְ הוּא לְזַכּוֹת אֶת יִשְׂרָאֵל, לְפִיכָךְ הִרְבָּה לָהֶם תּוֹרָה וּמִצְוֹת, שֶׁנֶּאֱמַר: "יהוה חָפֵץ לְמַעַן צִדְקוֹ, יַגְדִּיל תּוֹרָה וְיַאְדִּיר".

---

10. קָנָה — *Acquire (for Himself).* Of all the infinite universe, God singled out five things that uniquely advance the goals of creation.

תּוֹרָה — *Torah.* The Torah reveals God's will and purpose. Only by studying and obeying it can man fulfill the mission set forth for him by God.

שָׁמַיִם וָאָרֶץ — *Heaven and earth.* The domain on which Torah is to be fulfilled.

אַבְרָהָם — *Abraham.* The man who showed the way to the recognition of God.

יִשְׂרָאֵל — *Israel.* The Jewish people — bearers of the Covenant.

בֵּית הַמִּקְדָּשׁ — *The Holy Temple,* the "dwelling place" of the Divine Presence on this world.

11. After six chapters of teaching and exhortation, *Pirkei Avos* concludes with

6 *it shall guide you"* — in This World; *"when you lie down, it shall guard you"* — in the grave; *"and when you awake, it shall speak on your behalf"* — in the World to Come. And it says: *"Mine is the silver, and Mine is the gold, says* HASHEM, *Master of Legions"* (Chaggai 2:8).

[10] *Five possessions did the Holy One, Blessed is He, acquire [for Himself] in His world, and they are: Torah, one possession; heaven and earth, one possession; Abraham, one possession; Israel, one possession; the Holy Temple, one possession. From where do we know this about the Torah? Since it is written: "*HASHEM *acquired me [the Torah] at the beginning of His way, before His works in time of yore"* (Proverbs 8:22) *From where do we know this about heaven and earth? Since it is written: "So says* HASHEM. *The heaven is My throne, and the earth is My footstool; what House can you build for Me, and where is the place of My rest?"* (Isaiah 66:1). *And it says: "How abundant are Your works,* HASHEM, *with wisdom You made them all, the earth is full of Your possessions"* (Psalms 104:24). *From where do we know this about Abraham? Since it is written: "And He blessed him and said: Blessed is Abram of God the Most High, Who acquired heaven and earth"* (Genesis 14:19). *From where do we know this about the people Israel? Since it is written: "Until Your people passes through,* HASHEM, *until it passes through* — *this people You acquired"* (Exodus 15:16), *and it [also] says: "But for the holy ones who are in the earth and for the mighty all my desires are due to them"* (Psalms 16:3) *From where do we know this about the Holy Temple? Since it is written: "Your dwelling-place which You,* HASHEM, *have made; the Sanctuary, my Lord, that Your hands established"* (Exodus 15:17). *And it says: "And He brought them to His sacred boundary, to this mountain which His right hand acquired"* (Psalms 78:54).

[11] *All that the Holy One, Blessed is He, created in His world, He created solely for His glory, as it is said: "All that is called by My Name, indeed, it is for My glory that I have created it, formed it, and made it"* (Isaiah 43:7). *And it says: "*HASHEM *shall reign for all eternity"* (Exodus 15:18).

❧ ❧ ❧

Rabbi Chanania ben Akashia says: *The Holy One, Blessed is He, wished to confer merit upon Israel; therefore He gave them Torah and mitzvos in abundance, as it is said: "*HASHEM *desired, for the sake of its [Israel's] righteousness, that the Torah be made great and glorious"* (Isaiah 42:21).

---

the stirring and inspirational declaration that everything in creation is a tool for His glory. Clearly, since God created the universe for His service, no force can prevent man from utilizing it properly. God has shown us the way; it is for us to supply the will and the wisdom.

THE RABBIS' KADDISH / קדיש דרבנן

If a minyan *is present during recitation or study of* Pirkei Avos, *then one of them — a mourner, if one is present — recites* קדיש דרבנן, *the* Rabbi's Kaddish, *at the conclusion of the session.*

יִתְגַּדַּל וְיִתְקַדַּשׁ שְׁמֵהּ רַבָּא. (.Cong — אָמֵן) בְּעָלְמָא דִּי בְרָא כִרְעוּתֵהּ. וְיַמְלִיךְ מַלְכוּתֵהּ, בְּחַיֵּיכוֹן וּבְיוֹמֵיכוֹן וּבְחַיֵּי דְכָל בֵּית יִשְׂרָאֵל, בַּעֲגָלָא וּבִזְמַן קָרִיב. וְאִמְרוּ: אָמֵן.

(.Cong — אָמֵן. יְהֵא שְׁמֵהּ רַבָּא מְבָרַךְ לְעָלַם וּלְעָלְמֵי עָלְמַיָּא.)

יְהֵא שְׁמֵהּ רַבָּא מְבָרַךְ לְעָלַם וּלְעָלְמֵי עָלְמַיָּא.

יִתְבָּרַךְ וְיִשְׁתַּבַּח וְיִתְפָּאַר וְיִתְרוֹמַם וְיִתְנַשֵּׂא וְיִתְהַדָּר וְיִתְעַלֶּה וְיִתְהַלָּל שְׁמֵהּ דְּקֻדְשָׁא בְּרִיךְ הוּא (.Cong — בְּרִיךְ הוּא) — °לְעֵלָּא מִן כָּל בִּרְכָתָא וְשִׁירָתָא תֻּשְׁבְּחָתָא וְנֶחֱמָתָא, דַּאֲמִירָן בְּעָלְמָא. וְאִמְרוּ: אָמֵן. (.Cong — אָמֵן)

עַל יִשְׂרָאֵל וְעַל רַבָּנָן, וְעַל תַּלְמִידֵיהוֹן וְעַל כָּל תַּלְמִידֵי תַלְמִידֵיהוֹן, וְעַל כָּל מָאן דְּעָסְקִין בְּאוֹרַיְתָא, דִּי בְאַתְרָא הָדֵין וְדִי בְכָל אֲתַר וַאֲתַר. יְהֵא לְהוֹן וּלְכוֹן שְׁלָמָא רַבָּא, חִנָּא וְחִסְדָּא וְרַחֲמִין, וְחַיִּין אֲרִיכִין, וּמְזוֹנֵי רְוִיחֵי, וּפֻרְקָנָא מִן קֳדָם אֲבוּהוֹן דִּי בִשְׁמַיָּא (וְאַרְעָא). וְאִמְרוּ: אָמֵן. (.Cong — אָמֵן)

יְהֵא שְׁלָמָא רַבָּא מִן שְׁמַיָּא, וְחַיִּים (טוֹבִים) עָלֵינוּ וְעַל כָּל יִשְׂרָאֵל. וְאִמְרוּ: אָמֵן. (.Cong — אָמֵן)

עֹשֶׂה שָׁלוֹם בִּמְרוֹמָיו, הוּא בְּרַחֲמָיו יַעֲשֶׂה שָׁלוֹם עָלֵינוּ, וְעַל כָּל יִשְׂרָאֵל. וְאִמְרוּ: אָמֵן. (.Cong — אָמֵן)

יִתְגַּדַּל *May His great Name grow exalted and sanctified* (Cong. — *Amen.*) *in the world that He created as He willed. May He give reign to His kingship in your lifetimes and in your days, and in the lifetimes of the entire Family of Israel, swiftly and soon. Now respond: Amen.*

(Cong. — *Amen. May His great Name be blessed forever and ever.*)

May His great Name be blessed forever and ever.

Blessed, praised, glorified, exalted, extolled, mighty, upraised, and lauded be the Name of the Holy One, Blessed is He (Cong.— *Blessed is He*) *— beyond any blessing and song, praise and consolation that are uttered in the world. Now respond: Amen.* (Cong. — *Amen.*)

Upon Israel, upon the teachers, their disciples, and all of their disciples, and upon all those who engage in the study of Torah, who are here or anywhere else; may they and you have abundant peace, grace, kindness, and mercy, long life, ample nourishment, and salvation from before their Father Who is in Heaven (and on earth). Now respond: Amen. (Cong. — *Amen.*)

May there be abundant peace from Heaven, and (good) life, upon us and upon all Israel. Now respond: Amen. (Cong. — *Amen.*)

He Who makes peace in His heights, may He, in His compassion, make peace upon us, and upon all Israel. Now respond: Amen. (Cong. — *Amen.*)

ברכת המזון
Bircas hamazon

ברכת המזון

It is customary to recite Psalm 137, in memory of the Temple's destruction, before *Bircas HaMazon* on weekdays. On the Sabbath and Festivals, and on such occasions as the meals celebrating a marriage, *Bris*, or *Pidyon HaBen*, when it is improper to intrude upon the joy with memories of tragedy, Psalm 126, which describes the joy of redemption, is recited.

תהלים קלז

עַל נַהֲרוֹת בָּבֶל, שָׁם יָשַׁבְנוּ גַּם בָּכִינוּ, בְּזָכְרֵנוּ אֶת צִיּוֹן. עַל עֲרָבִים בְּתוֹכָהּ תָּלִינוּ כִּנֹּרוֹתֵינוּ. כִּי שָׁם שְׁאֵלוּנוּ שׁוֹבֵינוּ דִּבְרֵי שִׁיר וְתוֹלָלֵינוּ שִׂמְחָה, שִׁירוּ לָנוּ מִשִּׁיר צִיּוֹן. אֵיךְ נָשִׁיר אֶת שִׁיר יהוה, עַל אַדְמַת נֵכָר. אִם אֶשְׁכָּחֵךְ יְרוּשָׁלָיִם, תִּשְׁכַּח יְמִינִי. תִּדְבַּק לְשׁוֹנִי לְחִכִּי, אִם לֹא אֶזְכְּרֵכִי, אִם לֹא אַעֲלֶה אֶת יְרוּשָׁלַיִם עַל רֹאשׁ שִׂמְחָתִי. זְכֹר יהוה לִבְנֵי אֱדוֹם אֵת יוֹם יְרוּשָׁלָיִם, הָאֹמְרִים עָרוּ עָרוּ, עַד הַיְסוֹד בָּהּ. בַּת בָּבֶל הַשְּׁדוּדָה, אַשְׁרֵי שֶׁיְשַׁלֶּם לָךְ אֶת גְּמוּלֵךְ שֶׁגָּמַלְתְּ לָנוּ. אַשְׁרֵי שֶׁיֹּאחֵז וְנִפֵּץ אֶת עֹלָלַיִךְ אֶל הַסָּלַע.

תהלים קכו

שִׁיר הַמַּעֲלוֹת, בְּשׁוּב יהוה אֶת שִׁיבַת צִיּוֹן, הָיִינוּ כְּחֹלְמִים. אָז יִמָּלֵא שְׂחוֹק פִּינוּ וּלְשׁוֹנֵנוּ רִנָּה, אָז יֹאמְרוּ בַגּוֹיִם, הִגְדִּיל יהוה לַעֲשׂוֹת עִם אֵלֶּה. הִגְדִּיל יהוה לַעֲשׂוֹת עִמָּנוּ, הָיִינוּ שְׂמֵחִים. שׁוּבָה יהוה אֶת שְׁבִיתֵנוּ, כַּאֲפִיקִים בַּנֶּגֶב. הַזֹּרְעִים בְּדִמְעָה בְּרִנָּה יִקְצֹרוּ. הָלוֹךְ יֵלֵךְ וּבָכֹה נֹשֵׂא מֶשֶׁךְ הַזָּרַע, בֹּא יָבֹא בְרִנָּה, נֹשֵׂא אֲלֻמֹּתָיו.

תְּהִלַּת יהוה יְדַבֶּר פִּי, וִיבָרֵךְ כָּל בָּשָׂר שֵׁם קָדְשׁוֹ לְעוֹלָם וָעֶד.[1] וַאֲנַחְנוּ נְבָרֵךְ יָהּ, מֵעַתָּה וְעַד עוֹלָם, הַלְלוּיָהּ.[2] הוֹדוּ לַיהוה כִּי טוֹב, כִּי לְעוֹלָם חַסְדּוֹ.[3] מִי יְמַלֵּל גְּבוּרוֹת יהוה, יַשְׁמִיעַ כָּל תְּהִלָּתוֹ.[4]

הִנְנִי מוּכָן וּמְזֻמָּן לְקַיֵּם מִצְוַת עֲשֵׂה שֶׁל בִּרְכַּת הַמָּזוֹן, שֶׁנֶּאֱמַר: וְאָכַלְתָּ וְשָׂבָעְתָּ, וּבֵרַכְתָּ אֶת יהוה אֱלֹהֶיךָ, עַל הָאָרֶץ הַטֹּבָה אֲשֶׁר נָתַן לָךְ.[5]

ברכת המזון / GRACE AFTER MEALS

The commandment to thank God after a meal is of Scriptural origin: וְאָכַלְתָּ וְשָׂבָעְתָּ, וּבֵרַכְתָּ אֶת ה' אֱלֹהֶיךָ עַל הָאָרֶץ הַטֹּבָה אֲשֶׁר נָתַן לָךְ *And you shall eat and you shall be satisfied, and you shall bless HASHEM, your God, for the good land that He gave you* (Deuteronomy 8:10). As the verse indicates, the Scriptural requirement applies only when one has eaten his fill — *you shall eat and you shall be satisfied*. From earliest times, however, the Jewish people have undertaken to express its gratitude to God even after a modest meal, provided one had eaten at least as much bread as the volume of an olive (כְּזַיִת). There are several opinions regarding the modern

GRACE AFTER MEALS

It is customary to recite Psalm 137, in memory of the Temple's destruction, before *Bircas HaMazon* on weekdays. On the Sabbath and Festivals, and on such occasions as the meals celebrating a marriage, *Bris*, or *Pidyon HaBen*, when it is improper to intrude upon the joy with memories of tragedy, Psalm 126, which describes the joy of redemption, is recited.

Psalm 137

עַל נַהֲרוֹת *By the rivers of Babylon, there we sat and also wept when we remembered Zion. On the willows within it we hung our lyres. For there our captors requested words of song from us, with our lyres [playing] joyous music, "Sing for us from Zion's song!" "How can we sing the song of HASHEM upon the alien's soil?" If I forget you, O Jerusalem, let my right hand forget its skill. Let my tongue adhere to my palate, if I fail to recall you, if I fail to elevate Jerusalem above my foremost joy. Remember, HASHEM, for the offspring of Edom, the day of Jerusalem; for those who say, "Destroy! Destroy! to its very foundation." O violated daughter of Babylon, praiseworthy is he who repays you in accordance with the manner that you treated us. Praiseworthy is he who will clutch and dash your infants against the rock.*

Psalm 126

שִׁיר הַמַּעֲלוֹת *A song of ascents. When HASHEM will return the captivity of Zion, we will be like dreamers. Then our mouth will be filled with laughter and our tongue with glad song. Then they will declare among the nations, "HASHEM has done greatly with these." HASHEM has done greatly with us, we were gladdened. O HASHEM — return our captivity like springs in the desert. Those who tearfully sow will reap in glad song. He who bears the measure of seeds walks along weeping, but will return in exultation, a bearer of his sheaves.*

תְּהִלַּת *May my mouth declare the praise of HASHEM and may all flesh bless His Holy Name forever.*[1] *We will bless HASHEM from this time and forever, Halleluyah!*[2] *Give thanks to God for He is good, His kindness endures forever.*[3] *Who can express the mighty acts of HASHEM? Who can declare all His praise?*[4]

Behold I am prepared and ready to perform the positive commandment of Bircas HaMazon, for it is said: *"And you shall eat and you shall be satisfied and you shall bless HASHEM, your God, for the good land which He gave you."*[5]

---

(1) *Psalms* 145:21. (2) 115:18. (3) 118:1. (4) 106:2. (5) *Deuteronomy* 8:10.

---

equivalent of this Talmudic measurement; they range from one to one and four-fifths fluid ounces.

The first to compose a text for Grace After Meals was Moses, whose text is still recited as the first blessing of the Grace. Although Moses' blessing was composed in gratitude for the manna in the Wilderness, it makes no mention of the manna. It is equally noteworthy that the general commandment of Grace After Meals (cited above) was given in the context of a general exhortation to Israel that it remember the heavenly food with which God nourished it in the Wilderness. The message appears rather clear: When we thank God for giving us food, we are recognizing that there is no intrinsic difference between the manna and the livelihood one wrests from the earth through sweat and hard toil; both are gifts from heaven.

זימון

If three or more males, aged thirteen or older, participate in a meal, a leader is appointed to formally invite the others to join him in the recitation of *Bircas HaMazon*.

Leader — רַבּוֹתַי מִיר וֶועלֶען בֶּענְטְשֶׁען [רַבּוֹתַי נְבָרֵךְ].

Others — יְהִי שֵׁם יהוה מְבֹרָךְ מֵעַתָּה וְעַד עוֹלָם.¹

If ten men join in the *zimun*, the words in parentheses are added.

Leader — יְהִי שֵׁם יהוה מְבֹרָךְ* מֵעַתָּה וְעַד עוֹלָם.¹
בִּרְשׁוּת מָרָנָן וְרַבָּנָן וְרַבּוֹתַי, נְבָרֵךְ* (אֱלֹהֵינוּ*) שֶׁאָכַלְנוּ מִשֶּׁלוֹ.*

Others — בָּרוּךְ (אֱלֹהֵינוּ) שֶׁאָכַלְנוּ מִשֶּׁלוֹ וּבְטוּבוֹ חָיִינוּ.

Those who have not eaten respond:
בָּרוּךְ (אֱלֹהֵינוּ) וּמְבֹרָךְ שְׁמוֹ תָּמִיד לְעוֹלָם וָעֶד.

Leader — בָּרוּךְ (אֱלֹהֵינוּ) שֶׁאָכַלְנוּ מִשֶּׁלוֹ וּבְטוּבוֹ חָיִינוּ.

All — בָּרוּךְ הוּא וּבָרוּךְ שְׁמוֹ.

The *zimun* leader recites Grace After Meals (at least the first blessing and the conclusion of the others) aloud. Other than to respond *Amen* at the conclusion of each blessing, it is forbidden to interrupt Grace After Meals for any response other than those permitted during the *Shema*.

הברכה הראשונה – ברכת הזן

בָּרוּךְ אַתָּה יהוה אֱלֹהֵינוּ מֶלֶךְ הָעוֹלָם, הַזָּן אֶת הָעוֹלָם כֻּלּוֹ, בְּטוּבוֹ, בְּחֵן בְּחֶסֶד וּבְרַחֲמִים, הוּא נֹתֵן לֶחֶם לְכָל בָּשָׂר, כִּי לְעוֹלָם חַסְדּוֹ.² וּבְטוּבוֹ הַגָּדוֹל, תָּמִיד לֹא חָסַר לָנוּ, וְאַל יֶחְסַר לָנוּ מָזוֹן לְעוֹלָם וָעֶד. בַּעֲבוּר שְׁמוֹ הַגָּדוֹל,* כִּי הוּא אֵל זָן וּמְפַרְנֵס לַכֹּל, וּמֵטִיב* לַכֹּל, וּמֵכִין מָזוֹן לְכָל בְּרִיּוֹתָיו אֲשֶׁר בָּרָא. ❖ בָּרוּךְ אַתָּה יהוה, הַזָּן אֶת הַכֹּל. (**Others** – אָמֵן.)

◆§ זימון / Zimun (Invitation)

The word *zimun* connotes both *invitation* and *presentation*. When three or more people eat together, one *invites* the others to respond to his praise of God; and all of them jointly are required to *present themselves* as a group to come together in praise of God (based on *Berachos* 49b).

יְהִי שֵׁם ה׳ מְבֹרָךְ — *Blessed be the Name* . . . The leader, too, repeats the blessings because it would be improper and even sacrilegious for him to ask others to bless God while he, being part of the group, refrains from joining them (*Rashba*).

נְבָרֵךְ — *Let us bless.* A commandment done by an individual cannot be compared to one performed by a group. When three recite *Bircas HaMazon* together, they say נְבָרֵךְ, *let us bless;* ten say, נְבָרֵךְ אֱלֹהֵינוּ, *let us bless our God* . . . (*Berachos* 49b). A few who perform a commandment are far inferior to a multitude performing it (*Rashi, Lev.* 26:8). When many people unite to do God's will, each individual in the group reaches a far higher level than he would have had he acted alone, no matter how meritoriously (*Chofetz Chaim*).

שֶׁאָכַלְנוּ מִשֶּׁלוֹ — *He of Whose we have eaten.* This text is drawn from Abraham. He would invite wayfarers to his home and serve them lavishly. When they were sated and refreshed and ready to continue on their way,

ברכת המזון [68]

ZIMUN/INVITATION

If three or more males, aged thirteen or older, participate in a meal, a leader is appointed to formally invite the others to join him in the recitation of Grace After Meals.

Leader — *Gentlemen, let us bless.*

Others — *Blessed be the Name of HASHEM from this time and forever!*[1]

If ten men join in the *zimun*, the words in brackets are added.

Leader — *Blessed be the Name of HASHEM• from this time and forever!*[1]
*With the permission of the distinguished people present,
let us bless• [our God,] He of Whose we have eaten.•*

Others — *Blessed is [our God,] He of Whose we have eaten
and through Whose goodness we live.*

Those who have not eaten respond:
Blessed is He [our God] and blessed is His Name continuously forever.

Leader — *Blessed is [our God,] He of Whose we have eaten
and through Whose goodness we live.*

All — *Blessed is He and Blessed is His Name.*

The *zimun* leader recites Grace After Meals (at least the first blessing and the conclusion of the others) aloud. Other than to respond *Amen* at the conclusion of each blessing, it is forbidden to interrupt Grace After Meals for any response other than those permitted during the *Shema*.

FIRST BLESSING: FOR THE NOURISHMENT

בָּרוּךְ *Blessed are You, HASHEM, our God, King of the universe, Who nourishes the entire world, in His goodness — with grace, with kindness, and with mercy. He gives nourishment to all flesh, for His kindness is eternal.*[2] *And through His great goodness, we have never lacked, and may we never lack,• nourishment, for all eternity. For the sake of His Great Name,• because He is God Who nourishes and sustains all, and benefits• all, and He prepares food for all of His creatures which He has created.*

Leader — *Blessed are You, HASHEM, Who nourishes all.* (Others — *Amen.*)

---
(1) *Psalms* 113:2. (2) 136:25.

---

they would thank him. He would insist that their thanks should go not to him, but to God, the One from Whose bounty they had eaten (*Sotah* 10b; *Iyun Tefillah*).

בִּרְכַּת הַזָּן / Blessing for the Nourishment

Bircas HaMazon comprises four blessings, of which the first three are Scripturally ordained and the fourth was instituted by the Sages. The first blessing was, as noted above, composed by Moses in gratitude for the manna with which God sustained Israel daily in the desert (*Berachos* 48b). For that reason it precedes נוֹדֶה, *the Blessing for the Land,* even though it might seem more logical to thank God first for the land that produces food (*Bayis Chadash*).

תָּמִיד לֹא חָסֵר ... וְאַל יֶחְסַר — *Have never*

lacked . . . and may . . . never lack. The subject of the sentence is מָזוֹן, *nourishment*, and the verse expresses the prayer that just as food was never lacking in the desert, may it never be lacking in the future (*Etz Yosef*).

בַּעֲבוּר שְׁמוֹ הַגָּדוֹל — *For the sake of His Great Name.* We declare that the motive of our request for eternally abundant food is but for the sake of *His Great Name* so that we may be better able to serve Him; and we bless Him *because*...

זָן ... מְפַרְנֵס ... מֵטִיב — *Nourishes . . . sustains . . . benefits.* זָן, *nourishes,* refers to food; מֵטִיב, *benefits,* refers to shelter. מְפַרְנֵס, *sustains,* refers to clothing; These three phrases enumerate the basic needs of life, all of which are provided by God (*Etz Yosef*).

הברכה השנית – ברכת הארץ

נוֹדֶה לְךָ, יהוה אֱלֹהֵינוּ, עַל שֶׁהִנְחַלְתָּ לַאֲבוֹתֵינוּ* אֶרֶץ חֶמְדָּה טוֹבָה וּרְחָבָה.* וְעַל שֶׁהוֹצֵאתָנוּ יהוה אֱלֹהֵינוּ מֵאֶרֶץ מִצְרַיִם, וּפְדִיתָנוּ מִבֵּית עֲבָדִים, וְעַל בְּרִיתְךָ שֶׁחָתַמְתָּ בִּבְשָׂרֵנוּ,* וְעַל תּוֹרָתְךָ שֶׁלִּמַּדְתָּנוּ, וְעַל חֻקֶּיךָ שֶׁהוֹדַעְתָּנוּ, וְעַל חַיִּים חֵן וָחֶסֶד שֶׁחוֹנַנְתָּנוּ, וְעַל אֲכִילַת מָזוֹן שָׁאַתָּה זָן וּמְפַרְנֵס אוֹתָנוּ תָּמִיד, בְּכָל יוֹם וּבְכָל עֵת וּבְכָל שָׁעָה.

On Chanukah and Purim add the following.

(וְ)עַל הַנִּסִּים, וְעַל הַפֻּרְקָן, וְעַל הַגְּבוּרוֹת, וְעַל הַתְּשׁוּעוֹת, וְעַל הַמִּלְחָמוֹת, שֶׁעָשִׂיתָ לַאֲבוֹתֵינוּ בַּיָּמִים הָהֵם בַּזְּמַן הַזֶּה.

On Chanukah:

בִּימֵי מַתִּתְיָהוּ בֶּן יוֹחָנָן כֹּהֵן גָּדוֹל חַשְׁמוֹנָאִי וּבָנָיו, כְּשֶׁעָמְדָה מַלְכוּת יָוָן הָרְשָׁעָה עַל עַמְּךָ יִשְׂרָאֵל, לְהַשְׁכִּיחָם תּוֹרָתֶךָ, וּלְהַעֲבִירָם מֵחֻקֵּי רְצוֹנֶךָ. וְאַתָּה בְּרַחֲמֶיךָ הָרַבִּים, עָמַדְתָּ לָהֶם בְּעֵת צָרָתָם, רַבְתָּ אֶת רִיבָם, דַּנְתָּ אֶת דִּינָם, נָקַמְתָּ אֶת נִקְמָתָם.[1] מָסַרְתָּ גִּבּוֹרִים בְּיַד חַלָּשִׁים, וְרַבִּים בְּיַד מְעַטִּים, וּטְמֵאִים בְּיַד טְהוֹרִים, וּרְשָׁעִים בְּיַד צַדִּיקִים, וְזֵדִים בְּיַד עוֹסְקֵי תוֹרָתֶךָ. וּלְךָ עָשִׂיתָ שֵׁם גָּדוֹל וְקָדוֹשׁ בְּעוֹלָמֶךָ, וּלְעַמְּךָ יִשְׂרָאֵל עָשִׂיתָ תְּשׁוּעָה גְדוֹלָה[2] וּפֻרְקָן כְּהַיּוֹם הַזֶּה. וְאַחַר כֵּן בָּאוּ בָנֶיךָ לִדְבִיר בֵּיתֶךָ, וּפִנּוּ אֶת הֵיכָלֶךָ, וְטִהֲרוּ אֶת מִקְדָּשֶׁךָ, וְהִדְלִיקוּ נֵרוֹת בְּחַצְרוֹת קָדְשֶׁךָ, וְקָבְעוּ שְׁמוֹנַת יְמֵי חֲנֻכָּה אֵלּוּ, לְהוֹדוֹת וּלְהַלֵּל לְשִׁמְךָ הַגָּדוֹל.

On Purim:

בִּימֵי מָרְדְּכַי וְאֶסְתֵּר בְּשׁוּשַׁן הַבִּירָה, כְּשֶׁעָמַד עֲלֵיהֶם הָמָן הָרָשָׁע, בִּקֵּשׁ לְהַשְׁמִיד לַהֲרֹג וּלְאַבֵּד אֶת כָּל הַיְּהוּדִים, מִנַּעַר וְעַד זָקֵן, טַף וְנָשִׁים בְּיוֹם אֶחָד, בִּשְׁלוֹשָׁה עָשָׂר לְחֹדֶשׁ שְׁנֵים עָשָׂר, הוּא חֹדֶשׁ אֲדָר, וּשְׁלָלָם לָבוֹז.[3] וְאַתָּה בְּרַחֲמֶיךָ הָרַבִּים הֵפַרְתָּ אֶת עֲצָתוֹ, וְקִלְקַלְתָּ אֶת מַחֲשַׁבְתּוֹ, וַהֲשֵׁבוֹתָ לּוֹ גְּמוּלוֹ בְּרֹאשׁוֹ, וְתָלוּ אוֹתוֹ וְאֶת בָּנָיו עַל הָעֵץ.

בִּרְכַּת הָאָרֶץ ∻ / **Blessing for the Land**

The second blessing was also ordained by the Torah [*Deut. 8:10*, see *Overview* to ArtScroll *Bircas HaMazon*] and formulated by Joshua (*Berachos* 48a). He saw how much Moses wanted to enter *Eretz Yisrael*, and how anxious the Patriarchs were to be buried in it. Therefore when Joshua was privileged to enter it, he composed this blessing in its honor (*Shibolei HaLeket*).

The blessing begins and ends with thanks. The expression of gratitude refers to each of the enumerated items: the Land, the Exodus, the covenant, the Torah, the statutes, life, grace, kindness, and food.

שֶׁהִנְחַלְתָּ לַאֲבוֹתֵינוּ — *You have given to our forefathers as a heritage.* Eretz Yisrael is referred to as נַחֲלָה, *a heritage*, implying that it remains eternally our inheritance. Thus, the long exile means only that God denied us access to it in punishment for our sins, not that it ceased to be ours.

טוֹבָה וּרְחָבָה — *Good and spacious.* Whoever does not say that the Land is *desirable, good, and spacious* has not properly fulfilled his obligation [of *Bircas HaMazon*] (*Berachos* 48b); because, once the Torah required that the Land be mentioned, the Sages decreed that its praises, too, should be enumerated (*Talmidei R' Yonah*).

ברכת המזון [70]

SECOND BLESSING: FOR THE LAND

נוֹדֶה *We thank You, HASHEM, our God, because You have given to our forefathers as a heritage* a desirable, good and spacious* land; because You removed us, HASHEM, our God, from the land of Egypt and You redeemed us from the house of bondage; for Your covenant which You sealed in our flesh;* for Your Torah which You taught us and for Your statutes which You made known to us; for life, grace, and lovingkindness which You granted us; and for the provision of food with which You nourish and sustain us constantly, in every day, in every season, and in every hour.*

On Chanukah and Purim add the following.

(וְ)עַל *(And) for the miracles, and for the salvation, and for the mighty deeds, and for the victories, and for the battles which You performed for our forefathers in those days, at this time.*

On Chanukah:

בִּימֵי *In the days of Mattisyahu, the son of Yochanan, the High Priest, the Hasmonean, and his sons — when the wicked Greek kingdom rose up against Your people Israel to make them forget Your Torah and compel them to stray from the statutes of Your Will — You in Your great mercy stood up for them in the time of their distress. You took up their grievance, judged their cause, and avenged their wrong.*[1] *You delivered the strong into the hands of the weak, the many into the hands of the few, the impure into the hands of the pure, the wicked into the hands of the righteous, and the wanton into the hands of the diligent students of Your Torah. For Yourself You made a great and holy Name in Your world, and for Your people Israel You worked a great victory*[2] *and salvation as this very day. Thereafter, Your children came to the Holy of Holies of Your House, cleansed Your Temple, purified the site of Your Holiness and kindled lights in the Courtyards of Your Sanctuary; and they established these eight days of Chanukah to express thanks and praise to Your great Name.*

On Purim:

בִּימֵי *In the days of Mordechai and Esther, in Shushan, the capital, when Haman, the wicked, rose up against them and sought to destroy, to slay, and to exterminate all the Jews, young and old, infants and women, on the same day, on the thirteenth of the twelfth month which is the month of Adar, and to plunder their possessions.*[3] *But You, in Your abundant mercy, nullified his counsel and frustrated his intention and caused his design to return upon his own head and they hanged him and his sons on the gallows.*

---

(1) Cf. *Jeremiah* 51:36. (2) Cf. *I Samuel* 19:5. (3) *Esther* 3:13.

וְעַל בְּרִיתְךָ שֶׁחָתַמְתָּ בִּבְשָׂרֵנוּ — *(And) for Your covenant which You sealed in our flesh.* The reference is to circumcision, mention of which the Sages required in the blessing of the Land (*Berachos* 48b) because the Land was promised to Abraham in the merit of circumcision (*Genesis* 17:7-8).

Women are not subject to the commandments of circumcision and Torah study. Nevertheless, women do say, *for Your*

⋅§ If One Forgot to Recite עַל הַנִּסִּים on Chanukah and Purim.

If one realized his error before reaching the Name HASHEM of the next blessing (בָּרוּךְ אַתָּה ה׳, *Blessed are You,* HASHEM [p. 80]) he should go back to עַל הַנִּסִּים and continue from there.

If he has already recited the phrase בָּרוּךְ אַתָּה ה׳, *Blessed are You,* HASHEM, he continues to recite *Bircas HaMazon* until reaching the series of seasonal prayers which begin הָרַחֲמָן, *The compassionate One* (p. 86), and rectifies the omission as indicated there. If the omission is not discovered until after that point, nothing need be done.

---

[71] **GRACE AFTER MEALS**

וְעַל הַכֹּל, יהוה אֱלֹהֵינוּ, אֲנַחְנוּ מוֹדִים לָךְ וּמְבָרְכִים אוֹתָךְ, יִתְבָּרַךְ שִׁמְךָ בְּפִי כָּל חַי תָּמִיד לְעוֹלָם וָעֶד. כַּכָּתוּב, וְאָכַלְתָּ וְשָׂבָעְתָּ, וּבֵרַכְתָּ אֶת יהוה אֱלֹהֶיךָ, עַל הָאָרֶץ הַטֹּבָה אֲשֶׁר נָתַן לָךְ.¹ ❖ בָּרוּךְ אַתָּה יהוה, עַל הָאָרֶץ וְעַל הַמָּזוֹן. (Others – אָמֵן.)

הברכה השלישית – בנין ירושלים

רַחֵם יהוה אֱלֹהֵינוּ עַל יִשְׂרָאֵל עַמֶּךָ, וְעַל יְרוּשָׁלַיִם עִירֶךָ, וְעַל צִיּוֹן מִשְׁכַּן כְּבוֹדֶךָ, וְעַל מַלְכוּת בֵּית דָּוִד מְשִׁיחֶךָ,* וְעַל הַבַּיִת הַגָּדוֹל וְהַקָּדוֹשׁ שֶׁנִּקְרָא שִׁמְךָ עָלָיו. אֱלֹהֵינוּ אָבִינוּ, רְעֵנוּ זוּנֵנוּ פַּרְנְסֵנוּ וְכַלְכְּלֵנוּ וְהַרְוִיחֵנוּ, וְהַרְוַח לָנוּ יהוה אֱלֹהֵינוּ מְהֵרָה מִכָּל צָרוֹתֵינוּ. וְנָא אַל תַּצְרִיכֵנוּ, יהוה אֱלֹהֵינוּ, לֹא לִידֵי מַתְּנַת בָּשָׂר וָדָם, וְלֹא לִידֵי הַלְוָאָתָם, כִּי אִם לְיָדְךָ הַמְּלֵאָה הַפְּתוּחָה הַקְּדוֹשָׁה וְהָרְחָבָה, שֶׁלֹּא נֵבוֹשׁ וְלֹא נִכָּלֵם לְעוֹלָם וָעֶד.

On the Sabbath add the following. [If forgotten, see below.]

רְצֵה וְהַחֲלִיצֵנוּ יהוה אֱלֹהֵינוּ בְּמִצְוֹתֶיךָ, וּבְמִצְוַת יוֹם הַשְּׁבִיעִי הַשַּׁבָּת הַגָּדוֹל וְהַקָּדוֹשׁ הַזֶּה, כִּי יוֹם זֶה גָּדוֹל וְקָדוֹשׁ הוּא לְפָנֶיךָ, לִשְׁבָּת בּוֹ וְלָנוּחַ בּוֹ בְּאַהֲבָה כְּמִצְוַת רְצוֹנֶךָ, וּבִרְצוֹנְךָ הָנִיחַ לָנוּ יהוה אֱלֹהֵינוּ, שֶׁלֹּא תְהֵא צָרָה וְיָגוֹן וַאֲנָחָה בְּיוֹם מְנוּחָתֵנוּ, וְהַרְאֵנוּ יהוה אֱלֹהֵינוּ בְּנֶחָמַת צִיּוֹן עִירֶךָ, וּבְבִנְיַן יְרוּשָׁלַיִם עִיר קָדְשֶׁךָ, כִּי אַתָּה הוּא בַּעַל הַיְשׁוּעוֹת וּבַעַל הַנֶּחָמוֹת.

covenant which You sealed in our flesh; for Your Torah which You taught us. Magen Avraham explains that since women do not require circumcision, they are considered as equivalent to circumcised men in this regard; and since women must study the laws of whatever commandments are applicable to them, they have a share in the study of Torah.

◆◦§ בִּנְיַן יְרוּשָׁלַיִם / Blessing for Jerusalem

This blessing is the final one required by the Torah. It was composed in stages by David and Solomon. David, who occupied Jerusalem, referred to *Israel, Your people,* and *Jerusalem, Your city.* Solomon, after constructing the Temple, added, *the great and holy House* (Berachos 48b).

Their blessing was a prayer that God continue the tranquility of the Land. Following the destruction and exile, the blessing was changed to embody a prayer for the return of the Land, the Temple, and the Davidic dynasty. Before Joshua's conquest of the Land, the blessing took yet another form (*Tur*), a request for God's mercy upon the nation (*Aruch HaShulchan*).

וְעַל מַלְכוּת בֵּית דָּוִד מְשִׁיחֶךָ — *(And) on the monarchy of the house of David, Your anointed.* It is required that the monarchy of David's dynasty be mentioned in this bless-

וְעַל הַכּל *For all, HASHEM, our God, we thank You and bless You. May Your Name be blessed by the mouth of all the living, continuously for all eternity. As it is written: "And you shall eat and you shall be satisfied and you shall bless HASHEM, your God, for the good land which He gave you."*[1] *Leader—* Blessed are You, HASHEM, for the land and for the nourishment. (*Others—* Amen.)

THIRD BLESSING: FOR JERUSALEM

רַחֵם *Have mercy, HASHEM, our God, on Israel Your people; on Jerusalem, Your city; on Zion, the resting place of Your Glory; on the monarchy of the house of David, Your anointed;• and on the great and holy House upon which Your Name is called. Our God, our Father — tend us, nourish us, sustain us, support us, relieve us; HASHEM, our God, grant us speedy relief from all our troubles. Please, make us not needful — HASHEM, our God — of the gifts of human hands nor of their loans, but only of Your Hand that is full, open, holy, and generous, that we not feel inner shame nor be humiliated for ever and ever.*

> On the Sabbath add the following. [If forgotten, see below.]
>
> **רְצֵה** *May it please You, HASHEM, our God — give us rest through Your commandments and through the commandment of the seventh day, this great and holy Sabbath. For this day is great and holy before You to rest on it and be content on it in love, as ordained by Your will. May it be Your will, HASHEM, our God, that there be no distress, grief, or lament on this day of our contentment. And show us, HASHEM, our God, the consolation of Zion, Your city, and the rebuilding of Jerusalem, City of Your holiness, for You are the Master of salvations and Master of consolations.*

---

(1) *Deuteronomy* 8:10.

ing; whoever has not mentioned it has not fulfilled his obligation (*Berachos* 49a), because it was David who sanctified Jerusalem (*Rashi*); and because the consolation for the exile will not be complete until David's kingdom is restored (*Rambam*).

◆§ If One Omitted יַעֲלֶה וְיָבֹא or רְצֵה

a) If he realizes his omission after having recited the blessing of בּוֹנֵה, *Who rebuilds*, he makes up for the omission by reciting the appropriate Compensatory Blessing (p. 80).

b) If he realizes his omission after having recited the first six words of the fourth blessing, he may still switch immediately into the Compensatory Blessing since the words בָּרוּךְ אַתָּה . . . . הָעוֹלָם are identical in both blessings. (However, the Compensatory Blessing need not be recited after the third Sabbath meal if *Bircas HaMazon* is recited after sunset.)

c) If the omission is discovered after having recited the word הָאֵל, *the Almighty*, of the fourth blessing, it is too late for the Compensatory Blessing to be recited. In that case:

  (i) On the Sabbath and on a Festival day, at the first two meals *Bircas HaMazon* must be repeated in its entirety; at the third meal, nothing need be done.

  (ii) On Rosh Chodesh and on Chol HaMoed, nothing need be done except if the day fell on the Sabbath and רְצֵה, *Retzei*, was omitted. In that case, at the first two meals *Bircas HaMazon* must be repeated. But if רְצֵה was recited and יַעֲלֶה וְיָבֹא was omitted, nothing need be done.

On Rosh Chodesh, Chol HaMoed, and Festivals add. [If forgotten, see p. 73.]

אֱלֹהֵינוּ וֵאלֹהֵי אֲבוֹתֵינוּ, יַעֲלֶה, וְיָבֹא, וְיַגִּיעַ, וְיֵרָאֶה, וְיֵרָצֶה, וְיִשָּׁמַע, וְיִפָּקֵד, וְיִזָּכֵר, זִכְרוֹנֵנוּ וּפִקְדוֹנֵנוּ, וְזִכְרוֹן אֲבוֹתֵינוּ, וְזִכְרוֹן מָשִׁיחַ בֶּן דָּוִד עַבְדֶּךָ, וְזִכְרוֹן יְרוּשָׁלַיִם עִיר קָדְשֶׁךָ, וְזִכְרוֹן כָּל עַמְּךָ בֵּית יִשְׂרָאֵל לְפָנֶיךָ, לִפְלֵיטָה לְטוֹבָה לְחֵן וּלְחֶסֶד וּלְרַחֲמִים, לְחַיִּים וּלְשָׁלוֹם, בְּיוֹם

Rosh Chodesh: Pesach: Shavuos:

רֹאשׁ הַחֹדֶשׁ הַזֶּה.   חַג הַמַּצּוֹת הַזֶּה.   חַג הַשָּׁבֻעוֹת הַזֶּה.

Succos: Shemini Atzeres/Simchas Torah:

חַג הַסֻּכּוֹת הַזֶּה.   הַשְּׁמִינִי חַג הָעֲצֶרֶת הַזֶּה.

זָכְרֵנוּ יהוה אֱלֹהֵינוּ בּוֹ לְטוֹבָה, וּפָקְדֵנוּ בוֹ לִבְרָכָה, וְהוֹשִׁיעֵנוּ בוֹ לְחַיִּים. וּבִדְבַר יְשׁוּעָה וְרַחֲמִים, חוּס וְחָנֵּנוּ וְרַחֵם עָלֵינוּ וְהוֹשִׁיעֵנוּ, כִּי אֵלֶיךָ עֵינֵינוּ, כִּי אֵל (מֶלֶךְ) חַנּוּן וְרַחוּם אָתָּה.[1]

❖ **וּבְנֵה** יְרוּשָׁלַיִם עִיר הַקֹּדֶשׁ בִּמְהֵרָה בְיָמֵינוּ. בָּרוּךְ אַתָּה יהוה, בּוֹנֵה (בְרַחֲמָיו) יְרוּשָׁלָיִם. אָמֵן.

(אָמֵן. – Others)

[When required, the compensatory blessing (p. 80) is recited here.]

הברכה הרביעית – הטוב והמטיב

בָּרוּךְ אַתָּה יהוה אֱלֹהֵינוּ מֶלֶךְ הָעוֹלָם, הָאֵל אָבִינוּ מַלְכֵּנוּ אַדִּירֵנוּ בּוֹרְאֵנוּ גֹּאֲלֵנוּ יוֹצְרֵנוּ, קְדוֹשֵׁנוּ קְדוֹשׁ יַעֲקֹב, רוֹעֵנוּ רוֹעֵה יִשְׂרָאֵל, הַמֶּלֶךְ הַטּוֹב וְהַמֵּטִיב לַכֹּל, שֶׁבְּכָל יוֹם וָיוֹם* הוּא הֵטִיב, הוּא מֵטִיב, הוּא יֵיטִיב לָנוּ. הוּא גְמָלָנוּ הוּא גוֹמְלֵנוּ הוּא יִגְמְלֵנוּ לָעַד, לְחֵן וּלְחֶסֶד וּלְרַחֲמִים וּלְרֶוַח הַצָּלָה וְהַצְלָחָה, בְּרָכָה וִישׁוּעָה נֶחָמָה פַּרְנָסָה וְכַלְכָּלָה ❖ וְרַחֲמִים וְחַיִּים וְשָׁלוֹם וְכָל טוֹב, וּמִכָּל טוּב לְעוֹלָם אַל יְחַסְּרֵנוּ.*

(אָמֵן. – Others)

⋄§ **וּבְנֵה יְרוּשָׁלַיִם** — *Rebuild Jerusalem.* This concludes the third blessing, and thus returns to the theme with which the blessings began — a plea for God's mercy on Jerusalem (*Pesachim* 104a).

⋄§ **הַטּוֹב וְהַמֵּטִיב** / **Blessing for God's Goodness**

The essence of this blessing is the phrase הַטּוֹב וְהַמֵּטִיב, *Who is good and Who does good.* The court of Rabban Gamliel the Elder in Yavneh composed this blessing in gratitude to God for preserving the bodies of the victims of the Roman massacre at Betar, and for eventually allowing them to be brought to burial (*Berachos* 48b).

שֶׁבְּכָל יוֹם וָיוֹם — *For every single day.* It is

ברכת המזון [74]

On Rosh Chodesh, Chol HaMoed, and Festivals add. [If forgotten, see p. 73.]

אֱלֹהֵינוּ *Our God and God of our forefathers, may there rise, come, reach, be noted, be favored, be heard, be considered, and be remembered — the remembrance and consideration of ourselves; the remembrance of our forefathers; the remembrance of Messiah, son of David, Your servant; the remembrance of Jerusalem, the City of Your Holiness; and the remembrance of Your entire people the Family of Israel — before You for deliverance, for goodness, for grace, for kindness, and for compassion, for life, and for peace on this day of*

Rosh Chodesh:	Pesach:	Shavuos:
Rosh Chodesh.	*the Festival of Matzos.*	*the Shavuos Festival.*
Succos:	Shemini Atzeres/Simchas Torah:	
the Succos Festival.	*the Shemini Atzeres Festival.*	

Remember us on it, HASHEM, our God, for goodness; consider us on it for blessing; and help us on it for life. In the matter of salvation and compassion, pity, be gracious and compassionate with us and help us, for our eyes are turned to You, because You are God, the gracious and compassionate (King).[1]

וּבְנֵה Leader — *Rebuild Jerusalem, the Holy City, soon in our days. Blessed are You, HASHEM, Who rebuilds Jerusalem (in His mercy).*
Amen. (Others — Amen.)

[When required, the compensatory blessing (p. 80) is recited here.]

FOURTH BLESSING: GOD'S GOODNESS

בָּרוּךְ *Blessed are You, HASHEM, our God, King of the universe, the Almighty, our Father, our King, our Sovereign, our Creator, our Redeemer, our Maker, our Holy One, Holy One of Jacob, our Shepherd, the Shepherd of Israel, the King Who is good and Who does good for all. For every single day • He did good, He does good, and He will do good to us. He was bountiful with us, He is bountiful with us, and He will forever be bountiful with us — with grace and with kindness and with mercy, with relief, salvation, success, blessing, help, consolation, sustenance, support,* Leader — *mercy, life, peace, and all good; and of all good things may He never deprive us.* •
(Others — Amen.)

---

(1) Cf. *Nehemiah* 9:31.

insufficient to thank God for His graciousness to *past* generations. We must be conscious of the fact that His goodness and bounty occur constantly.

אַל יְחַסְּרֵנוּ — *May He never deprive us.* This is the conclusion of the fourth blessing. Unlike the other parts of *Bircas HaMazon*, this one does not conclude with a brief blessing summing up the theme of the section. As noted above, the essential text of the blessing consists of only two words — הַטּוֹב וְהַמֵּטִיב, *Who is good and Who does good* — and it is therefore no different from the short blessings recited before performing a commandment or partaking of food. The addition to the text of considerable outpourings of gratitude does not alter the fact that the brief text does not call for a double blessing (*Rashi* to *Berachos* 49a).

הָרַחֲמָן הוּא יִמְלוֹךְ עָלֵינוּ לְעוֹלָם וָעֶד. הָרַחֲמָן הוּא יִתְבָּרַךְ בַּשָּׁמַיִם וּבָאָרֶץ. הָרַחֲמָן הוּא יִשְׁתַּבַּח לְדוֹר דּוֹרִים, וְיִתְפָּאַר בָּנוּ לָעַד וּלְנֵצַח נְצָחִים, וְיִתְהַדַּר בָּנוּ לָעַד וּלְעוֹלְמֵי עוֹלָמִים.* הָרַחֲמָן הוּא יְפַרְנְסֵנוּ בְּכָבוֹד. הָרַחֲמָן הוּא יִשְׁבּוֹר עֻלֵּנוּ מֵעַל צַוָּארֵנוּ, וְהוּא יוֹלִיכֵנוּ קוֹמְמִיּוּת לְאַרְצֵנוּ. הָרַחֲמָן הוּא יִשְׁלַח לָנוּ בְּרָכָה מְרֻבָּה בַּבַּיִת הַזֶּה, וְעַל שֻׁלְחָן זֶה שֶׁאָכַלְנוּ עָלָיו. הָרַחֲמָן הוּא יִשְׁלַח לָנוּ אֶת אֵלִיָּהוּ הַנָּבִיא זָכוּר לַטּוֹב,* וִיבַשֶּׂר לָנוּ בְּשׂוֹרוֹת טוֹבוֹת יְשׁוּעוֹת וְנֶחָמוֹת.

The following is a blessing that a guest inserts here for the host.

יְהִי רָצוֹן שֶׁלֹּא יֵבוֹשׁ וְלֹא יִכָּלֵם בַּעַל הַבַּיִת הַזֶּה, לֹא בָּעוֹלָם הַזֶּה וְלֹא בָּעוֹלָם הַבָּא, וְיַצְלִיחַ בְּכָל נְכָסָיו, וְיִהְיוּ נְכָסָיו מֻצְלָחִים וּקְרוֹבִים לָעִיר, וְאַל יִשְׁלוֹט שָׂטָן בְּמַעֲשֵׂה יָדָיו, וְאַל יִזְדַּקֵּק לְפָנָיו שׁוּם דְּבַר חֵטְא וְהִרְהוּר עָוֹן, מֵעַתָּה וְעַד עוֹלָם.

Guests recite the following (children at their parents' table include the applicable words in parentheses):

הָרַחֲמָן הוּא יְבָרֵךְ אֶת (אָבִי מוֹרִי) בַּעַל הַבַּיִת הַזֶּה, וְאֶת (אִמִּי מוֹרָתִי) בַּעֲלַת הַבַּיִת הַזֶּה, אוֹתָם וְאֶת בֵּיתָם וְאֶת זַרְעָם וְאֶת כָּל אֲשֶׁר לָהֶם.

At one's own table (include the applicable words in parentheses):

הָרַחֲמָן הוּא יְבָרֵךְ אוֹתִי (וְאֶת אִשְׁתִּי / וְאֶת בַּעְלִי. וְאֶת זַרְעִי) וְאֶת כָּל אֲשֶׁר לִי.

אוֹתָנוּ וְאֶת כָּל אֲשֶׁר לָנוּ, כְּמוֹ שֶׁנִּתְבָּרְכוּ אֲבוֹתֵינוּ אַבְרָהָם יִצְחָק וְיַעֲקֹב בַּכֹּל מִכֹּל כֹּל,*[1] כֵּן יְבָרֵךְ אוֹתָנוּ כֻּלָּנוּ יַחַד בִּבְרָכָה שְׁלֵמָה. וְנֹאמַר: אָמֵן.

בַּמָּרוֹם יְלַמְּדוּ עֲלֵיהֶם* וְעָלֵינוּ* זְכוּת, שֶׁתְּהֵא לְמִשְׁמֶרֶת שָׁלוֹם.* וְנִשָּׂא בְרָכָה מֵאֵת יהוה, וּצְדָקָה מֵאֱלֹהֵי יִשְׁעֵנוּ, וְנִמְצָא חֵן וְשֵׂכֶל טוֹב בְּעֵינֵי אֱלֹהִים וְאָדָם.[2]

⁕ הָרַחֲמָן — *The compassionate One!* After completing the four blessings of *Bircas HaMazon* we recite a collection of brief prayers for God's compassion.

לָנֵצַח נְצָחִים . . . לְעוֹלְמֵי עוֹלָמִים — *To the ultimate ends . . . for all eternity.* These expressions mean "forever" and are essentially synonymous. Our translation is based on R' Hirsch who renders נֵצַח from נִצָּחוֹן, *triumph*, for God's plan for the future will ultimately overcome all barriers. The word עוֹלָם is related to נֶעְלָם, *hidden*, implying that the hand of God is present in all occurrences, even though it seems to be hidden.

זָכוּר לַטּוֹב — *He is remembered for good.* The Sages use this generic term to refer to people who have rendered great and unforgettable service to the entire Jewish nation

הָרַחֲמָן *The compassionate One! May He reign over us forever. The compassionate One! May He be blessed in heaven and on earth. The compassionate One! May He be praised throughout all generations, may He be glorified through us forever to the ultimate ends, and be honored through us forever and for all eternity.* The compassionate One! May He sustain us in honor. The compassionate One! May He break the yoke of oppression from our necks and guide us erect to our Land. The compassionate One! May He send us abundant blessing to this house and upon this table at which we have eaten. The compassionate One! May He send us Elijah, the Prophet — he is remembered for good* — to proclaim to us good tidings, salvations, and consolations.*

> The following is a blessing that a guest inserts here for the host.
>
> **יְהִי** *May it be God's will that this host not be shamed nor humiliated in This World or in the World to Come. May he be successful in all his dealings. May his dealings be successful and conveniently close at hand. May no evil impediment reign over his handiwork, and may no semblance of sin or iniquitous thought attach itself to him from this time and forever.*

At one's own table (include the applicable words in parentheses):	Guests recite the following (children at their parents' table include the applicable words in parentheses):
The compassionate One! May He bless me (my wife/husband and my children) and all that is mine.	*The compassionate One! May He bless (my father, my teacher) the master of this house, and (my mother, my teacher) lady of this house, them, their house, their family, and all that is theirs.*

Ours and all that is ours — just as our forefathers Abraham, Isaac, and Jacob were blessed in everything, from everything, with everything.*¹ So may He bless us all together with a perfect blessing. And let us say: Amen!

בַּמָּרוֹם *On high, may merit be pleaded upon them* and upon us,* for a safeguard of peace.* May we receive a blessing from HASHEM and just kindness from the God of our salvation, and find favor and good understanding in the eyes of God and man.* ²

---

(1) Cf. *Genesis* 24:1; 27:33; 33:11. (2) Cf. *Proverbs* 3:4.

(see *Berachos* 3a, *Shabbos* 13b, *Bava Basra* 21a, *Avodah Zarah* 8b). In addition to the service he rendered during his years on earth, Elijah will herald the arrival of Messiah [*Malachi* 3:23] (*Iyun Tefillah*).

בְּכֹל מִכֹּל כֹּל — *In everything, from everything, with everything.* The three expressions, each indicating that no necessary measure of goodness was lacking, are used respectively by the Torah referring to the three Patriarchs.

עֲלֵיהֶם — *Upon them,* i.e., the master and mistress of the home, or any others who were mentioned in the preceding prayer.

וְעָלֵינוּ — *And upon us,* i.e., all gathered around the table. [When one eats alone, this term refers to whatever people were previously specified and to the Jewish people in general.]

לְמִשְׁמֶרֶת שָׁלוֹם — *For a safeguard of peace,* i.e., to assure that the home will be peaceful.

If any of the following verses was omitted, *Bircas HaMazon* need not be repeated.

On the Sabbath add:

הָרַחֲמָן הוּא יַנְחִילֵנוּ יוֹם שֶׁכֻּלּוֹ שַׁבָּת* וּמְנוּחָה לְחַיֵּי הָעוֹלָמִים.

On Rosh Chodesh add:

הָרַחֲמָן הוּא יְחַדֵּשׁ עָלֵינוּ אֶת הַחֹדֶשׁ הַזֶּה לְטוֹבָה וְלִבְרָכָה.

On Festivals add:

הָרַחֲמָן הוּא יַנְחִילֵנוּ יוֹם שֶׁכֻּלּוֹ טוֹב.

On Succos add:

הָרַחֲמָן הוּא יָקִים לָנוּ אֶת סֻכַּת דָּוִיד הַנֹּפֶלֶת.[1]

On Chanukah and Purim, if *Al HaNissim* was not recited in its proper place, add:

הָרַחֲמָן הוּא יַעֲשֶׂה לָנוּ נִסִּים וְנִפְלָאוֹת
כַּאֲשֶׁר עָשָׂה לַאֲבוֹתֵינוּ בַּיָּמִים הָהֵם בַּזְּמַן הַזֶּה.

Continue בִּימֵי (p. 70).

הָרַחֲמָן הוּא יְזַכֵּנוּ לִימוֹת הַמָּשִׁיחַ וּלְחַיֵּי הָעוֹלָם הַבָּא. [מַגְדִּיל* – on weekdays / מִגְדּוֹל* – on days *Mussaf* is recited] יְשׁוּעוֹת מַלְכּוֹ וְעֹשֶׂה חֶסֶד לִמְשִׁיחוֹ לְדָוִד וּלְזַרְעוֹ עַד עוֹלָם.[2] עֹשֶׂה שָׁלוֹם בִּמְרוֹמָיו,* הוּא יַעֲשֶׂה שָׁלוֹם עָלֵינוּ וְעַל כָּל יִשְׂרָאֵל. וְאִמְרוּ, אָמֵן.

יְראוּ אֶת יהוה* קְדֹשָׁיו, כִּי אֵין מַחְסוֹר לִירֵאָיו. כְּפִירִים רָשׁוּ וְרָעֵבוּ, וְדֹרְשֵׁי יהוה לֹא יַחְסְרוּ כָל טוֹב.[3] הוֹדוּ לַיהוה כִּי טוֹב, כִּי לְעוֹלָם חַסְדּוֹ.[4] פּוֹתֵחַ אֶת יָדֶךָ, וּמַשְׂבִּיעַ לְכָל חַי רָצוֹן.[5] בָּרוּךְ הַגֶּבֶר אֲשֶׁר יִבְטַח בַּיהוה, וְהָיָה יהוה מִבְטַחוֹ.[6]* נַעַר הָיִיתִי גַּם זָקַנְתִּי, וְלֹא רָאִיתִי צַדִּיק נֶעֱזָב, וְזַרְעוֹ מְבַקֶּשׁ לָחֶם.[7]* יהוה עֹז לְעַמּוֹ יִתֵּן, יהוה יְבָרֵךְ אֶת עַמּוֹ בַשָּׁלוֹם.[8]*

יוֹם שֶׁכֻּלּוֹ שַׁבָּת — *The day which will be completely a Sabbath,* an allusion to the World to Come after the final redemption.

מַגְדִּיל/מִגְדּוֹל ఈ— *He Who makes great/A tower.* Both of these verses were written by King David and, in the context of *Bircas HaMazon*, the word *king* refers to King Messiah. *Etz Yosef* explains that the phrase from Psalms [מַגְדִּיל] was chosen for the less holy weekdays because it was written before David became king. The phrase from

Samuel [מִגְדּוֹל] was composed when David was at the peak of his greatness, and it is therefore more suited to the Sabbath and festivals.

עֹשֶׂה שָׁלוֹם בִּמְרוֹמָיו — *He Who makes peace in His heights.* Even the heavenly beings require God to make peace among them, how much more so fractious man! (*Etz Yosef*).

יְראוּ אֶת ה׳ — *Fear HASHEM.* Those who fear God are content, even if they are lacking in

[78] ברכת המזון

If any of the following verses was omitted, *Bircas HaMazon* need not be repeated.

On the Sabbath add:
The compassionate One! May He cause us to inherit the day which will be completely a Sabbath* and rest day for eternal life.

On Rosh Chodesh add:
The compassionate One! May He inaugurate this month upon us for goodness and for blessing.

On Festivals add:
The compassionate One! May He cause us to inherit the day which is completely good.

On Succos add:
The compassionate One! May He erect for us David's fallen booth. [1]

On Chanukah and Purim, if *Al HaNissim* was not recited in its proper place, add:
The compassionate One! May He perform for us miracles and wonders as He performed for our forefathers in those days, at this time.

Continue "*In the days of . . .*" (p. 70).

הָרַחֲמָן *The compassionate One! May He make us worthy of the days of Messiah and the life of the World to Come.*

on weekdays: *He Who makes great* the salvations of His king*
on days *Mussaf* is recited: *He Who is a tower* of salvations to His king and does kindness for His anointed, to David and to his descendants forever.* [2] *He Who makes peace in His heights,* may He make peace upon us and upon all Israel. Now respond: Amen!*

יְראוּ *Fear HASHEM,* you — His holy ones — for there is no deprivation for His reverent ones. Young lions may want and hunger, but those who seek HASHEM will not lack any good.* [3] *Give thanks to God for He is good; His kindness endures forever.* [4] *You open Your hand and satisfy the desire of every living thing.* [5] *Blessed is the man who trusts in HASHEM, then HASHEM will be his security.* *[6] *I was a youth and also have aged, and I have not seen a righteous man forsaken, with his children begging for bread.* *[7] *HASHEM will give might to His people; HASHEM will bless His people with peace.* *[8]

---

(1) Cf. *Amos* 9:11. (2) *Psalms* 18:51. (3) 34:10-11. (4) 136:1 et al.
(5) 145:16. (6) *Jeremiah* 17:7. (7) *Psalms* 37:25. (8) 29:11.

---

material possessions. But the wicked are never satisfied; whatever they have only whets their appetite for more (*Anaf Yosef*).

אֲשֶׁר יִבְטַח בַּה׳ וְהָיָה ה׳ מִבְטַחוֹ — *Who trusts in HASHEM, then HASHEM will be his security.* God will be a fortress of trust to a man in direct proportion to the amount of trust he places in God (*Chidushei HaRim*).

צַדִּיק נֶעֱזָב וְזַרְעוֹ מְבַקֶּשׁ לָחֶם — *A righteous man forsaken, with his children begging for bread.* A righteous man may suffer misfortune, but God will surely have mercy on His children (*Radak; Malbim*). I have never seen a righteous man consider himself forsaken even if his children must beg for bread. Whatever his lot in life, he trusts that God

ברכות למי ששכח

See below for instances when Compensatory Blessings must be recited. In all cases, the conclusion of the blessing is recited only at the first two meals of the Sabbath and/or Festivals (except Chol HaMoed). After the appropriate blessing, continue with the fourth blessing (p. 74).

If one forgot רְצֵה on the Sabbath:

בָּרוּךְ אַתָּה יהוה אֱלֹהֵינוּ מֶלֶךְ הָעוֹלָם, אֲשֶׁר נָתַן שַׁבָּתוֹת לִמְנוּחָה לְעַמּוֹ יִשְׂרָאֵל בְּאַהֲבָה, לְאוֹת וְלִבְרִית. בָּרוּךְ אַתָּה יהוה, מְקַדֵּשׁ הַשַּׁבָּת.

If one forgot יַעֲלֶה וְיָבֹא on Rosh Chodesh:

בָּרוּךְ אַתָּה יהוה אֱלֹהֵינוּ מֶלֶךְ הָעוֹלָם, אֲשֶׁר נָתַן רָאשֵׁי חֳדָשִׁים לְעַמּוֹ יִשְׂרָאֵל לְזִכָּרוֹן.

If one forgot רְצֵה and יַעֲלֶה וְיָבֹא on Rosh Chodesh that falls on the Sabbath:

בָּרוּךְ אַתָּה יהוה אֱלֹהֵינוּ מֶלֶךְ הָעוֹלָם, אֲשֶׁר נָתַן שַׁבָּתוֹת לִמְנוּחָה לְעַמּוֹ יִשְׂרָאֵל בְּאַהֲבָה, לְאוֹת וְלִבְרִית, וְרָאשֵׁי חֳדָשִׁים לְזִכָּרוֹן. בָּרוּךְ אַתָּה יהוה, מְקַדֵּשׁ הַשַּׁבָּת וְיִשְׂרָאֵל וְרָאשֵׁי חֳדָשִׁים.

If one forgot יַעֲלֶה וְיָבֹא on a Festival:

בָּרוּךְ אַתָּה יהוה אֱלֹהֵינוּ מֶלֶךְ הָעוֹלָם, אֲשֶׁר נָתַן יָמִים טוֹבִים לְעַמּוֹ יִשְׂרָאֵל לְשָׂשׂוֹן וּלְשִׂמְחָה, אֶת יוֹם

Pesach   Shavuos   Succos   Shemini Atzeres / Simchas Torah

חַג הַמַּצּוֹת / חַג הַשָּׁבֻעוֹת / חַג הַסֻּכּוֹת / הַשְּׁמִינִי חַג הָעֲצֶרֶת הַזֶּה. בָּרוּךְ אַתָּה יהוה, מְקַדֵּשׁ יִשְׂרָאֵל וְהַזְּמַנִּים.

If one forgot יַעֲלֶה וְיָבֹא and רְצֵה on a Festival that falls on the Sabbath:

בָּרוּךְ אַתָּה יהוה אֱלֹהֵינוּ מֶלֶךְ הָעוֹלָם, אֲשֶׁר נָתַן שַׁבָּתוֹת לִמְנוּחָה לְעַמּוֹ יִשְׂרָאֵל בְּאַהֲבָה, לְאוֹת וְלִבְרִית, וְיָמִים טוֹבִים לְשָׂשׂוֹן וּלְשִׂמְחָה, אֶת יוֹם

Pesach   Shavuos   Succos   Shemini Atzeres / Simchas Torah

חַג הַמַּצּוֹת / חַג הַשָּׁבֻעוֹת / חַג הַסֻּכּוֹת / הַשְּׁמִינִי חַג הָעֲצֶרֶת הַזֶּה. בָּרוּךְ אַתָּה יהוה, מְקַדֵּשׁ הַשַּׁבָּת וְיִשְׂרָאֵל וְהַזְּמַנִּים.

If one forgot יַעֲלֶה וְיָבֹא on Chol HaMoed:

בָּרוּךְ אַתָּה יהוה אֱלֹהֵינוּ מֶלֶךְ הָעוֹלָם, אֲשֶׁר נָתַן מוֹעֲדִים לְעַמּוֹ יִשְׂרָאֵל לְשָׂשׂוֹן וּלְשִׂמְחָה, אֶת יוֹם *on Pesach* – חַג הַמַּצּוֹת / *on Succos* – חַג הַסֻּכּוֹת] הַזֶּה.

If one forgot יַעֲלֶה וְיָבֹא and רְצֵה on the Sabbath of Chol HaMoed:

בָּרוּךְ אַתָּה יהוה אֱלֹהֵינוּ מֶלֶךְ הָעוֹלָם, אֲשֶׁר נָתַן שַׁבָּתוֹת לִמְנוּחָה לְעַמּוֹ יִשְׂרָאֵל בְּאַהֲבָה, לְאוֹת וְלִבְרִית, וּמוֹעֲדִים לְשָׂשׂוֹן וּלְשִׂמְחָה, אֶת יוֹם [*on Pesach* – חַג הַמַּצּוֹת / *on Succos* – חַג הַסֻּכּוֹת] הַזֶּה. בָּרוּךְ אַתָּה יהוה, מְקַדֵּשׁ הַשַּׁבָּת וְיִשְׂרָאֵל וְהַזְּמַנִּים.

---

brings it upon him for a constructive and merciful purpose (*Anaf Yosef*).

The verse does not say that no righteous man would ever be reduced to poverty; were that the case, it would equate poverty with wickedness — a patent falsehood.

⋄{ COMPENSATORY BLESSINGS }⋄

See below for instances when Compensatory Blessings must be recited. In all cases, the conclusion of the blessing is recited only at the first two meals of the Sabbath and/or Festivals (except Chol HaMoed). After the appropriate blessing, continue with the fourth blessing (p. 74).

If one forgot רְצֵה on the Sabbath:

בָּרוּךְ *Blessed are You, HASHEM, our God, King of the universe, Who gave Sabbaths for contentment to His people Israel with love, for a sign and a covenant. Blessed are You, HASHEM, Who sanctifies the Sabbath.*

If one forgot יַעֲלֶה וְיָבֹא on Rosh Chodesh:

בָּרוּךְ *Blessed are You, HASHEM, our God, King of the universe, Who gave New Moons to His people Israel as a remembrance.*

If one forgot רְצֵה and יַעֲלֶה וְיָבֹא on Rosh Chodesh that falls on the Sabbath:

בָּרוּךְ *Blessed are You, HASHEM, our God, King of the universe, Who gave Sabbaths for contentment to His people Israel with love, for a sign and a covenant, and New Moons for a remembrance. Blessed are You, HASHEM, Who sanctifies the Sabbath, Israel, and New Moons.*

If one forgot יַעֲלֶה וְיָבֹא on a Festival:

בָּרוּךְ *Blessed are You, HASHEM, our God, King of the universe, Who gave festivals to His people Israel for happiness and gladness, this festival day of Matzos / Shavuos / Succos / Shemini Atzeres.*
Blessed are You, HASHEM, Who sanctifies Israel and the seasons.

If one forgot רְצֵה and יַעֲלֶה וְיָבֹא on a Festival that falls on the Sabbath:

בָּרוּךְ *Blessed are You, HASHEM, our God, King of the universe, Who gave Sabbaths for contentment to His people Israel with love, for a sign and a covenant, and festivals for happiness and gladness, this festival day of Matzos / Shavuos / Succos / Shemini Atzeres.*
Blessed are You, HASHEM, Who sanctifies the Sabbath, Israel, and the seasons.

If one forgot יַעֲלֶה וְיָבֹא on Chol HaMoed:

בָּרוּךְ *Blessed are You, HASHEM, our God, King of the universe, Who appointed festivals to His people Israel for happiness and gladness, this festival day of [Matzos /Succos].*

If one forgot רְצֵה and יַעֲלֶה וְיָבֹא on the Sabbath of Chol HaMoed:

בָּרוּךְ *Blessed are You, HASHEM, our God, King of the universe, Who gave Sabbaths for contentment to His people Israel with love, for a sign and a covenant, and appointed festivals for happiness and gladness, this festival day of [Matzos / Succos]. Blessed are You, HASHEM, Who sanctifies the Sabbath, Israel, and the (festive) seasons.*

Rather the verse says that no righteous person will be completely forsaken even if he must beg alms for his sustenance. Since Jews are obligated to help one another, it is no disgrace for one to require the help of another (*R' Hirsch*).

בְּשָׁלוֹם — *With peace.* Rabbi Shimon ben Chalafta said: The Holy One, Blessed is He, could find no container which would hold Israel's blessings as well as peace, as it says: "HASHEM *will give might to His people,* HASHEM *will bless His people with peace*" (*Uktzin* 3:12). The blessing of peace is so vital that the word שָׁלוֹם, *peace*, concludes the Oral Law (ibid.), the final blessing of *Shemoneh Esrei*, the *Priestly Blessings*, and *Bircas HaMazon*. It is also the essential word in our greetings to one another.

ברכות אחרונות

מעין שלש

The following blessing is recited after partaking of: (a) grain products (other than bread or matzah) made from wheat, barley, rye, oats, or spelt; (b) grape wine or grape juice; (c) grapes, figs, pomegranates, olives, or dates. (If foods from two or three of these groups were eaten, then the insertions for each group are connected with the conjunctive ו, thus וְעַל. The order in such a case is grain, wine, fruit.)

בָּרוּךְ אַתָּה יהוה אֱלֹהֵינוּ מֶלֶךְ הָעוֹלָם, עַל

After grain products:	After wine:	After fruits:
הָעֵץ וְעַל פְּרִי הָעֵץ,	הַגֶּפֶן וְעַל פְּרִי הַגֶּפֶן,	הַמִּחְיָה וְעַל הַכַּלְכָּלָה,

וְעַל תְּנוּבַת הַשָּׂדֶה, וְעַל אֶרֶץ חֶמְדָּה טוֹבָה וּרְחָבָה, שֶׁרָצִיתָ וְהִנְחַלְתָּ לַאֲבוֹתֵינוּ, לֶאֱכֹל מִפִּרְיָהּ וְלִשְׂבֹּעַ מִטּוּבָהּ. רַחֶם נָא יהוה אֱלֹהֵינוּ עַל יִשְׂרָאֵל עַמֶּךָ, וְעַל יְרוּשָׁלַיִם עִירֶךָ, וְעַל צִיּוֹן מִשְׁכַּן כְּבוֹדֶךָ, וְעַל מִזְבְּחֶךָ וְעַל הֵיכָלֶךָ. וּבְנֵה יְרוּשָׁלַיִם עִיר הַקֹּדֶשׁ בִּמְהֵרָה בְיָמֵינוּ, וְהַעֲלֵנוּ לְתוֹכָהּ, וְשַׂמְּחֵנוּ בְּבִנְיָנָהּ, וְנֹאכַל מִפִּרְיָהּ, וְנִשְׂבַּע מִטּוּבָהּ, וּנְבָרֶכְךָ עָלֶיהָ בִּקְדֻשָּׁה וּבְטָהֳרָה.

— On the Sabbath — וּרְצֵה וְהַחֲלִיצֵנוּ בְּיוֹם הַשַּׁבָּת הַזֶּה.
— On Rosh Chodesh — וְזָכְרֵנוּ (לְטוֹבָה) בְּיוֹם רֹאשׁ הַחֹדֶשׁ הַזֶּה.
— On Pesach — וְשַׂמְּחֵנוּ בְּיוֹם חַג הַמַּצּוֹת הַזֶּה.
— On Shavuos — וְשַׂמְּחֵנוּ בְּיוֹם חַג הַשָּׁבֻעוֹת הַזֶּה.
— On Succos — וְשַׂמְּחֵנוּ בְּיוֹם חַג הַסֻּכּוֹת הַזֶּה.
— On Shemini Atzeres / Simchas Torah — וְשַׂמְּחֵנוּ בְּיוֹם הַשְּׁמִינִי חַג הָעֲצֶרֶת הַזֶּה.

כִּי אַתָּה יהוה טוֹב וּמֵטִיב לַכֹּל, וְנוֹדֶה לְךָ עַל הָאָרֶץ וְעַל

After grain products:	After wine:	After fruits:
הַמִּחְיָה (וְעַל הַכַּלְכָּלָה).	פְּרִי הַגֶּפֶן.°	הַפֵּרוֹת.°°

בָּרוּךְ אַתָּה יהוה, עַל הָאָרֶץ וְעַל

הַמִּחְיָה (וְעַל הַכַּלְכָּלָה).	פְּרִי הַגֶּפֶן.°	הַפֵּרוֹת.°°

°If the wine is from *Eretz Yisrael*, substitute גַּפְנָהּ for הַגֶּפֶן.
°°If the fruit grew in *Eretz Yisrael*, substitute פֵּירוֹתֶיהָ for הַפֵּרוֹת.

בורא נפשות

After eating or drinking any food to which neither *Bircas HaMazon* nor the Three-Faceted Blessing applies, such as fruits other than the above, vegetables, or beverages other than wine, recite:

בָּרוּךְ אַתָּה יהוה אֱלֹהֵינוּ מֶלֶךְ הָעוֹלָם, בּוֹרֵא נְפָשׁוֹת רַבּוֹת וְחֶסְרוֹנָן, עַל כָּל מַה שֶּׁבָּרָא(תָ) לְהַחֲיוֹת בָּהֶם נֶפֶשׁ כָּל חָי. בָּרוּךְ חֵי הָעוֹלָמִים.

◄{ BLESSINGS AFTER OTHER FOODS }►

THE THREE-FACETED BLESSING

The following blessing is recited after partaking of: (a) grain products (other than bread or matzah) made from wheat, barley, rye, oats, or spelt; (b) grape wine or grape juice; (c) grapes, figs, pomegranates, olives, or dates. (If foods from two or three of these groups were eaten, then the insertions for each group are connected with the conjunctive ו, thus וְעַל. The order in such a case is grain, wine, fruit.)

בָּרוּךְ *Blessed are You, HASHEM, our God, King of the universe, for the*

After grain products:	After wine:	After fruits:
nourishment and the sustenance,	vine and the fruit of the vine,	tree and the fruit of the tree,

and for the produce of the field; for the desirable, good, and spacious Land that You were pleased to give our forefathers as a heritage, to eat of its fruit and to be satisfied with its goodness. Have mercy, we beg You, HASHEM, our God, on Israel Your people; on Jerusalem, Your city; on Zion, the resting place of Your glory; on Your Altar, and on Your Temple. Rebuild Jerusalem the city of holiness, speedily in our days. Bring us up into it and gladden us in its rebuilding and let us eat from its fruit and be satisfied with its goodness and bless You upon it in holiness and purity.

On the Sabbath:	*And be pleased to let us rest on this Sabbath day.*
On Rosh Chodesh:	*And remember us (for goodness) on this day of Rosh Chodesh.*
On Pesach:	*And gladden us on this day of the festival of Matzos.*
On Shavuos:	*And gladden us on this day of the festival of Shavuos.*
On Succos:	*And gladden us on this day of the festival of Succos.*
On Shemini Atzeres and Simchas Torah:	*And gladden us on this day of the festival of Shemini Atzeres.*

For You, HASHEM, are good and do good to all and we thank You for the land and for the

After grain products:	After wine:	After fruits:
nourishment (and the sustenance).	fruit of the vine. °	fruit. ° °

Blessed are You, HASHEM, for the land and for the

nourishment (and the sustenance).	fruit of the vine. °	fruit. ° °

°*If the wine is from* Eretz Yisrael, *substitute "its wine."*
°°*If the fruit grew in* Eretz Yisrael, *substitute "its fruit."*

BOREI NEFASHOS

After eating or drinking any food to which neither the Grace After Meals nor the Three-Faceted Blessing applies, such as fruits other than the above, vegetables, or beverages other than wine, recite:

בָּרוּךְ *Blessed are You, HASHEM, our God, King of the universe, Who creates numerous living things with their deficiencies; for all that You have created with which to maintain the life of every being. Blessed is He, the life of the worlds.*

◆§ סדר ברכות אירוסין ונישואין §◆

When the groom reaches the *chupah*, the *chazzan* sings:

בָּרוּךְ הַבָּא. מִי אַדִּיר עַל הַכֹּל, מִי בָּרוּךְ עַל הַכֹּל, מִי גָּדוֹל עַל הַכֹּל, מִי דָּגוּל עַל הַכֹּל, הוּא יְבָרֵךְ אֶת הֶחָתָן וְאֶת הַכַּלָּה.

As the bride approaches the *chupah*, the groom should take a step or two forward in greeting. She then circles the groom, according to the custom, and the *chazzan* sings:

בְּרוּכָה הַבָּאָה. מִי בֶן שִׂיחַ שׁוֹשַׁן חוֹחִים, אַהֲבַת כַּלָּה מְשׂוֹשׂ דּוֹדִים, הוּא יְבָרֵךְ אֶת הֶחָתָן וְאֶת הַכַּלָּה.

The *mesader kiddushin* holds a cup of wine and recites:

בָּרוּךְ אַתָּה יהוה אֱלֹהֵינוּ מֶלֶךְ הָעוֹלָם, בּוֹרֵא פְּרִי הַגָּפֶן.

בָּרוּךְ אַתָּה יהוה אֱלֹהֵינוּ מֶלֶךְ הָעוֹלָם, אֲשֶׁר קִדְּשָׁנוּ בְּמִצְוֹתָיו, וְצִוָּנוּ עַל הָעֲרָיוֹת, וְאָסַר לָנוּ אֶת הָאֲרוּסוֹת, וְהִתִּיר לָנוּ אֶת הַנְּשׂוּאוֹת לָנוּ עַל יְדֵי חֻפָּה וְקִדּוּשִׁין. בָּרוּךְ אַתָּה יהוה, מְקַדֵּשׁ עַמּוֹ יִשְׂרָאֵל עַל יְדֵי חֻפָּה וְקִדּוּשִׁין.

Groom and bride each drink from the wine. The groom holds his ring ready to place upon the bride's right index finger and says to her:

הֲרֵי אַתְּ מְקֻדֶּשֶׁת לִי, בְּטַבַּעַת זוֹ, כְּדַת מֹשֶׁה וְיִשְׂרָאֵל.

After the ring is placed on the bride's finger, the *kesubah* (marriage contract) is read aloud and handed to the groom who presents it to the bride. Then a second cup of wine is poured and seven blessings (שֶׁבַע בְּרָכוֹת) are recited aloud. First the blessing over wine is recited and then blessings 1-6 on p. 86. The honor of reciting these seven blessings may be divided among several people, but the first two should be recited by the same person. After the blessings, both groom and bride drink from the wine. The groom then smashes a glass with his right foot to symbolize that until the Temple is rebuilt our joy cannot be complete. This act concludes the public marriage service. Then the groom and bride must spend some time together in a completely private room.

◆§ זימון לשבע ברכות §◆

When *Sheva Berachos* are recited, the leader recites the following *zimun*, with a cup of wine in hand.

– Leader — רַבּוֹתַי מִיר וֶועלֶען בֶּענְטְשֶׁען [רַבּוֹתַי נְבָרֵךְ].
– Others — יְהִי שֵׁם יהוה מְבֹרָךְ מֵעַתָּה וְעַד עוֹלָם.
– Leader — יְהִי שֵׁם יהוה מְבֹרָךְ מֵעַתָּה וְעַד עוֹלָם. דְּוַי הָסֵר וְגַם חָרוֹן, וְאָז אִלֵּם בְּשִׁיר יָרוֹן, נְחֵנוּ בְּמַעְגְּלֵי צֶדֶק, שְׁעֵה בִּרְכַּת בְּנֵי אַהֲרֹן. בִּרְשׁוּת מָרָנָן וְרַבָּנָן וְרַבּוֹתַי, נְבָרֵךְ אֱלֹהֵינוּ שֶׁהַשִּׂמְחָה בִמְעוֹנוֹ, (וְ)שֶׁאָכַלְנוּ מִשֶּׁלּוֹ.
– Others — בָּרוּךְ אֱלֹהֵינוּ שֶׁהַשִּׂמְחָה בִמְעוֹנוֹ, (וְ)שֶׁאָכַלְנוּ מִשֶּׁלּוֹ וּבְטוּבוֹ חָיִינוּ.
– Leader — בָּרוּךְ אֱלֹהֵינוּ שֶׁהַשִּׂמְחָה בִמְעוֹנוֹ, (וְ)שֶׁאָכַלְנוּ מִשֶּׁלּוֹ וּבְטוּבוֹ חָיִינוּ.
– All — בָּרוּךְ הוּא וּבָרוּךְ שְׁמוֹ.

Continue with *Bircas HaMazon*, p. 68.

⚜ THE MARRIAGE SERVICE ⚜

When the groom reaches the *chupah*, the *chazzan* sings:

בָּרוּךְ הַבָּא *Blessed is he who has come! He Who is powerful above all, He Who is blessed above all, He Who is great above all, He Who is supreme above all* — *may He bless the groom and bride.*

As the bride approaches the *chupah*, the groom should take a step or two forward in greeting. She then circles the groom, according to the custom, and the *chazzan* sings:

בְּרוּכָה הַבָּאָה *Blessed is she who has come! He Who understands the speech of the rose among the thorns, the love of a bride, who is the joy of the beloved ones* — *may He bless the groom and bride.*

The *mesader kiddushin* holds a cup of wine and recites:

בָּרוּךְ *Blessed are You, Hashem, our God, King of the universe, Who creates the fruit of the vine.* (All — *Amen.*)

בָּרוּךְ *Blessed are You, Hashem, our God, King of the universe, Who has sanctified us with His commandments, and has commanded us regarding forbidden unions; Who forbade betrothed women to us, and permitted women who are married to us through canopy and consecration. Blessed are You, Hashem, Who sanctified His people Israel through canopy and consecration.* (All — *Amen.*)

Groom and bride each drink from the wine. The groom holds his ring ready to place upon the bride's right index finger and says to her:

Behold, you are consecrated to me by means of this ring, according to the ritual of Moses and Israel.

After the ring is placed on the bride's finger, the *kesubah* (marriage contract) is read aloud and handed to the groom who presents it to the bride. Then a second cup of wine is poured and seven blessings (שֶׁבַע בְּרָכוֹת) are recited aloud. First the blessing over wine is recited and then blessings 1-6 on p. 86. The honor of reciting these seven blessings may be divided among several people, but the first two should be recited by the same person. After the blessings, both groom and bride drink from the wine. The groom then smashes a glass with his right foot to symbolize that until the Temple is rebuilt our joy cannot be complete. This act concludes the public marriage service. Then the groom and bride must spend some time together in a completely private room.

⚜ ZIMUN FOR SHEVA BERACHOS ⚜

When *Sheva Berachos* are recited, the leader recites the following *zimun*, with a cup of wine in hand.

Leader — *Gentlemen, let us bless.*

Others — *Blessed be the Name of* HASHEM *from this time and forever!*

Leader — *Blessed be the Name of* HASHEM *from this time and forever!*
Banish pain and also wrath, and then the mute will exult in song. Guide us in the paths of righteousness, heed the blessing of the children of Aaron. With the permission of the distinguished people present, let us bless our God, in Whose abode is this celebration, of Whose we have eaten.

Others — *Blessed is our God, in Whose abode is this celebration, of Whose we have eaten and through Whose goodness we live.*

Leader — *Blessed is our God, in Whose abode is this celebration, of Whose we have eaten and through Whose goodness we live.*

All — *Blessed is He and Blessed is His Name.*

Continue with *Bircas HaMazon*, p. 68.

❧ שבע ברכות ❧

After *Bircas HaMazon* a second cup is poured and the following seven blessings are recited.
They may be recited by one person or divided among several people.
Whoever recites a blessing should hold the cup as he does so.

1. **בָּרוּךְ** אַתָּה יהוה אֱלֹהֵינוּ מֶלֶךְ הָעוֹלָם, שֶׁהַכֹּל בָּרָא לִכְבוֹדוֹ. (All – אָמֵן.)

2. **בָּרוּךְ** אַתָּה יהוה אֱלֹהֵינוּ מֶלֶךְ הָעוֹלָם, יוֹצֵר הָאָדָם. (All – אָמֵן.)

3. **בָּרוּךְ** אַתָּה יהוה אֱלֹהֵינוּ מֶלֶךְ הָעוֹלָם, אֲשֶׁר יָצַר אֶת הָאָדָם בְּצַלְמוֹ, בְּצֶלֶם דְּמוּת תַּבְנִיתוֹ, וְהִתְקִין לוֹ מִמֶּנּוּ בִּנְיַן עֲדֵי עַד. בָּרוּךְ אַתָּה יהוה, יוֹצֵר הָאָדָם. (All – אָמֵן.)

4. **שׂוֹשׂ** תָּשִׂישׂ וְתָגֵל הָעֲקָרָה, בְּקִבּוּץ בָּנֶיהָ לְתוֹכָהּ בְּשִׂמְחָה. בָּרוּךְ אַתָּה יהוה, מְשַׂמֵּחַ צִיּוֹן בְּבָנֶיהָ. (All – אָמֵן.)

5. **שַׂמֵּחַ** תְּשַׂמַּח רֵעִים הָאֲהוּבִים, כְּשַׂמֵּחֲךָ יְצִירְךָ בְּגַן עֵדֶן מִקֶּדֶם. בָּרוּךְ אַתָּה יהוה, מְשַׂמֵּחַ חָתָן וְכַלָּה. (All – אָמֵן.)

6. **בָּרוּךְ** אַתָּה יהוה אֱלֹהֵינוּ מֶלֶךְ הָעוֹלָם, אֲשֶׁר בָּרָא שָׂשׂוֹן וְשִׂמְחָה, חָתָן וְכַלָּה, גִּילָה רִנָּה, דִּיצָה וְחֶדְוָה, אַהֲבָה וְאַחֲוָה, וְשָׁלוֹם וְרֵעוּת. מְהֵרָה, יהוה אֱלֹהֵינוּ, יִשָּׁמַע בְּעָרֵי יְהוּדָה וּבְחֻצוֹת יְרוּשָׁלָיִם, קוֹל שָׂשׂוֹן וְקוֹל שִׂמְחָה, קוֹל חָתָן וְקוֹל כַּלָּה, קוֹל מִצְהֲלוֹת חֲתָנִים מֵחֻפָּתָם, וּנְעָרִים מִמִּשְׁתֵּה נְגִינָתָם. בָּרוּךְ אַתָּה יהוה, מְשַׂמֵּחַ חָתָן עִם הַכַּלָּה. (All – אָמֵן.)

The leader of *Bircas HaMazon* recites the seventh blessing:

7. **בָּרוּךְ** אַתָּה יהוה אֱלֹהֵינוּ מֶלֶךְ הָעוֹלָם, בּוֹרֵא פְּרִי הַגָּפֶן. (All – אָמֵן.)

The leader drinks some of the wine from his cup; then wine from the two cups is mixed together and one cup is given to the groom and the other to the bride. It is laudable for those present to drink a bit of wine from the כּוֹס שֶׁל בְּרָכָה, *Cup of Blessing*, since it was used in the performance of a *mitzvah*.

◈§ SHEVA BERACHOS §◈

After *Bircas HaMazon* a second cup is poured and the following seven blessings are recited.
They may be recited by one person or divided among several people.
Whoever recites a blessing should hold the cup as he does so.

1. **בָּרוּךְ** *Blessed are You, HASHEM, our God, King of the universe, Who has created everything for His glory.* (All— Amen.)

2. **בָּרוּךְ** *Blessed are You, HASHEM, our God, King of the universe, Who fashioned the Man.* (All— Amen.)

3. **בָּרוּךְ** *Blessed are You, HASHEM, our God, King of the universe, Who fashioned the Man in His image, in the image of his likeness, and prepared for him — from himself — a building for eternity. Blessed are You, HASHEM, Who fashioned the Man.* (All— Amen.)

4. **שׂוֹשׂ** *Bring intense joy and exultation to the barren one through the ingathering of her children amidst her in gladness. Blessed are You, HASHEM, Who gladdens Zion through her children.*

    (All— Amen.)

5. **שַׂמֵּחַ** *Gladden the beloved companions as You gladdened Your creature in the Garden of Eden from aforetime. Blessed are You, HASHEM, Who gladdens groom and bride.* (All— Amen.)

6. **בָּרוּךְ** *Blessed are You, HASHEM, our God, King of the universe, Who created joy and gladness, groom and bride, mirth, glad song, pleasure, delight, love, brotherhood, peace, and companionship. HASHEM, our God, let there soon be heard in the cities of Judah and the streets of Jerusalem the sound of joy and the sound of gladness, the voice of the groom and the voice of the bride, the sound of the grooms' jubilance from their canopies and of youths from their song-filled feasts. Blessed are You, Who gladdens the groom with the bride.* (All— Amen.)

The leader of *Bircas HaMazon* recites the seventh blessing:

7. **בָּרוּךְ** *Blessed are You, HASHEM, our God, King of the universe, Who creates the fruit of the vine.* (All— Amen.)

The leader drinks some of the wine from his cup; then wine from the two cups is mixed together and one cup is given to the groom and the other to the bride. It is laudable for those present to drink a bit of wine from the כּוֹס שֶׁל בְּרָכָה, *Cup of Blessing,* since it was used in the performance of a *mitzvah*.

⊰ WAYFARER'S PRAYER / תפלת הדרך ⊱

When setting out on a journey one recites this prayer once he leaves the city limits.

יְהִי רָצוֹן מִלְּפָנֶיךָ, יהוה אֱלֹהֵינוּ וֵאלֹהֵי אֲבוֹתֵינוּ, שֶׁתּוֹלִיכֵנוּ לְשָׁלוֹם, וְתַצְעִידֵנוּ לְשָׁלוֹם, וְתַדְרִיכֵנוּ לְשָׁלוֹם. וְתַגִּיעֵנוּ לִמְחוֹז חֶפְצֵנוּ לְחַיִּים וּלְשִׂמְחָה וּלְשָׁלוֹם,

יְהִי May it be Your will, HASHEM, our God and the God of our forefathers, that You lead us toward peace, emplace our footsteps toward peace, guide us toward peace, and make us reach our desired destination for life, gladness, and peace,

one who is planning to return on the same day adds:

and return us to our homes in peace.

וְתַחֲזִירֵנוּ לְבֵיתֵנוּ לְשָׁלוֹם,

May You rescue us from the hand of every foe, ambush, (bandits, and evil animals) along the way, and from all manner of punishments that assemble to come to earth. May You send blessing in our (every) handiwork, and grant us grace, kindness, and mercy in Your eyes and in the eyes of all who see us. May You hear the sound of our supplication, because You are God Who hears prayer and supplication. Blessed are You, HASHEM, Who hears prayer.

וְתַצִּילֵנוּ מִכַּף כָּל אוֹיֵב וְאוֹרֵב וְלִסְטִים וְחַיּוֹת רָעוֹת בַּדֶּרֶךְ, וּמִכָּל מִינֵי פֻּרְעָנִיּוֹת הַמִּתְרַגְּשׁוֹת לָבוֹא לָעוֹלָם, וְתִשְׁלַח בְּרָכָה בְּכָל מַעֲשֵׂה יָדֵינוּ, וְתִתְּנֵנוּ לְחֵן וּלְחֶסֶד וּלְרַחֲמִים בְּעֵינֶיךָ וּבְעֵינֵי כָל רוֹאֵינוּ, וְתִשְׁמַע קוֹל תַּחֲנוּנֵינוּ, כִּי אֵל שׁוֹמֵעַ תְּפִלָּה וְתַחֲנוּן אָתָּה. בָּרוּךְ אַתָּה יהוה, שׁוֹמֵעַ תְּפִלָּה.

The following verses are recited three times each:

Jacob went on his way and angels of God encountered him. Jacob said when he saw them, 'This is a Godly camp.' So he named the place Machanayim. [1]

וְיַעֲקֹב הָלַךְ לְדַרְכּוֹ, וַיִּפְגְּעוּ בוֹ מַלְאֲכֵי אֱלֹהִים. וַיֹּאמֶר יַעֲקֹב כַּאֲשֶׁר רָאָם, מַחֲנֵה אֱלֹהִים זֶה, וַיִּקְרָא שֵׁם הַמָּקוֹם הַהוּא מַחֲנָיִם.[1]

For Your salvation I do long, HASHEM. [2] *I do long, HASHEM, for Your salvation. HASHEM, for Your salvation I do long.*

לִישׁוּעָתְךָ קִוִּיתִי יהוה.[2] (קִוִּיתִי יהוה לִישׁוּעָתְךָ. יהוה לִישׁוּעָתְךָ קִוִּיתִי.

Behold I send an angel before you to protect you on the way and to bring you to the place that I have prepared. [3]

הִנֵּה אָנֹכִי שֹׁלֵחַ מַלְאָךְ לְפָנֶיךָ לִשְׁמָרְךָ בַּדֶּרֶךְ, וְלַהֲבִיאֲךָ אֶל הַמָּקוֹם אֲשֶׁר הֲכִנֹתִי.[3]

HASHEM will give might to His nation, HASHEM will bless His nation with peace. [4]

יהוה עֹז לְעַמּוֹ יִתֵּן, יהוה יְבָרֵךְ אֶת עַמּוֹ בַשָּׁלוֹם.[4]

(1) *Genesis* 32:2-3. (2) 49:18. (3) *Exodus* 23:20. (4) *Psalms* 29:11.